turn back your
age
CLOCK

hamlyn

turn back your

age

CLOCK

look and feel 20 years younger in only 8 weeks

TIM BEAN & ANNE LAING

An Hachette Livre UK Company
www.hachettelivre.co.uk

First published in Great Britain in 2009 by
Hamlyn, a division of Octopus Publishing Group Ltd
2–4 Heron Quays, London E14 4JP
www.octopusbooks.co.uk
www.octopusbooksusa.com

Distributed in the U.S. and Canada by Octopus Books USA:
c/o Hachette Book Group USA
237 Park Avenue
New York NY 10017

ISBN 978-0-600-61717-4

A CIP catalogue record for this book is
available from the British Library

Printed and bound in China

10 9 8 7 6 5 4 3 2 1

Note

While the advice and information in this book is believed to be accurate, neither the
author nor the publisher will be responsible for any injury, losses, damages, actions,
proceedings, claims, demands, expenses and costs incurred in any way arising out
of following the exercises in this book.

This book is not intended to take the place of medical advice from a qualified
doctor. We recommend that readers consult a qualified health professional
before implementing any of the suggestions and techniques in this book. Neither
the publisher nor the author takes any responsibility for any action, activity or
administration of medicine or other application by anyone reading or following
the instructions in this book.

Contents

Introduction

The American comedian and actor George Burns once said: 'You know you're getting old when you stoop to tie your shoelaces and wonder what else you could do while you're down there.' We say: 'Don't get older, get better!' No one yet knows exactly why people age, but we do know more about the things we do that age us faster. So take some time out to learn the tips and secrets we have enclosed in this book to turn back your own age clock.

Our philosophy is that you only have one body to take you through life, so it's worth making an effort to get to grips with how it works and how to look after it early on in the process. It is false economy to be 'too busy' to take care of your most amazing asset. After years of study and working with thousands of clients, we now know there is no magical age at which someone suddenly becomes, or starts behaving, 'old'. It is generally self-determined, and is definitely not a slope that each person falls down at the same rate, if at all. Everyone can change – it's never too late!

We have developed an immense admiration for the restorative mechanics of our bodies. In observing the exercise, nutrition and lifestyle habits of thousands of individuals ranging from 10 to 100, we have seen that it doesn't matter what your eating habits are, or how slow your metabolism has become. In every case, our clients have been able to turn things around. Their pay-off is not just that they will live longer, but they will live longer, better and younger!

This book is meant both to inform you and to act as your guide, helping you follow a path in the best direction we know how in order to 'de-age' your body – a launching pad, if you like, towards allowing you to live better and for longer.

Tim Bean and Anne Laing

How to use this book

This book is designed to help you focus on areas that need attention in order to turn back your age clock. It provides tests to help you assess your biological age and devotes chapters to looking after your skin, diet and weight, and exercise. There is also a chapter dedicated to getting and keeping you motivated. The master plan pulls everything together into an age-busting eight-week plan.

• First take a few moments to understand what your biological age is and what ages you (see page 8).

• Test yourself to find your biological age (see Test Your Real Age, pages 26–41).

• Turn to The Master Plan (see pages 42–53). This is the most important section of the book. Every week of the plan details which exercises you should do each day, referring you to the relevant pages in the Anti-aging Workout chapter, and directs you to dietary and skin-care advice in the chapters dedicated to these topics. It also suggests ways to maintain a healthier lifestyle and each week has a tip to help you on your way to a younger you.

• Refer to the Super Skin chapter (see pages 54–65) for advice on looking after your outer layer and for a step-by-step DIY lymphatic massage.

• Refer regularly to the common myths (see page 9) and make sure you don't fall into the trap of believing them. Motivation is extremely important (see page 17).

SAFETY NOTE

Get a full medical from your GP or health advisor before you start – it's essential to get their clearance before commencing on any new regime of exercise or nutrition.

Age is only a number

Aging is an all-encompassing term for a combination of factors that influence every cell, hormone and organ in the body. It is also an ongoing active process of physical health, nutritional well-being, intellectual stimuli, social interaction and emotional and purposeful existence.

We all have a chronological age, which measures how many years have passed since we were born. Our biological age tells us what sort of health condition we are in for the number of years we have been around. In other words, one tells us how long we've been alive, the other tells us how long we've left to live.

We accelerate the aging process by overeating nutritionally empty foods, undereating foods rich in nutrients and by neglecting to exercise in a way that keeps our bodies fit and strong. There is also a tendency to adopt a mantle of 'oldness' too early in life by giving up activity, challenge and adventure.

It is never too late to turn back your age clock and regain a youthful vitality and physique. As with anything worthwhile, it takes extra dedication and persistence to be successful, but that little extra makes all the difference between ordinary and extraordinary aging. Taking 20 years off your age clock might seem like an ambitious promise, but the plan really does work!

The tests on pages 28–41 will help you to assess your biological age. You may find that your biological age is greater in some areas than others, but remember you can lose up to 20 years from your age clock in just eight weeks. For example, you may be 32 years old, but the results of the majority of these tests show that your biological age is nearer 45. By following the programme in this book, after eight weeks you will have turned your 'real' age clock back by 20 years to a youthful 25!

SOME COMMON MYTHS

'I am too busy/tired to cook at home.'
Comment: We teach our clients to cook meals by the '10-minute rule' – meals that only take 10 minutes from start to finish. There isn't a takeaway you can order out in that time and it is seldom possible to get your restaurant meal to the table in half an hour, let alone 10 minutes!

'Why should I worry, as we are living longer now than ever before?'
Comment: Yes, we are living longer now, but not necessarily healthier, and the outlook isn't so good for the coming generations saddled with our legacy of out-of-control heart disease, cancer, diabetes and obesity. Turning back your age clock is about being in a state of total quality well-being, physically and psychologically, and not having every body function propped up by medication.

'I just don't have the time to exercise or eat properly.'
Comment: Do you always somehow make time for things like picking up children from school, paying the bills or going out to dinner? As the saying goes, 'If you don't make time for health now, you will surely have to make time for illness later.' Don't look at time spent on your body as a chore, or a negative investment. Consider exercise as a daily 'hygiene routine'. You need to do it every day giving it equal importance to eating, washing your hair or taking a shower.

'I am an emotional and a comfort eater.'
Comment: 'Comfort foods' are designed to keep you wanting more. They taste and smell wonderful, but they come without any of the nutrition your metabolism needs. When you eat, chemicals are stimulated to produce enzymes to break food down for the repair and maintenance of your body and brain. If these expected nutrients don't arrive, you quickly feel emotionally and physically empty again, but the calories have already been tucked away in the fat cells and the cycle starts over. Willpower is not the issue – it is being knowledgeable and prepared.

'I find exercise boring.'
Comment: Life is full of boring things, such as cleaning your teeth, taking the train to work, driving the kids to school. What makes boring things worthwhile are the results you get at the end. The trick is to find ways to make the necessary boring things a little more interesting. Thomas Jefferson said: 'Nothing can stop the man with the right mental attitude from achieving his goal. Nothing on earth can help the man with the wrong mental attitude.'

'I am this weight because of my genes.'
Comment: Genes only play a tiny part in your weight. Our gene pool has changed only a minuscule amount in the last 10,000 years. The truth is that you choose how fat or fit your own body becomes, because it is completely and totally made up of what you eat and how you exercise.

'I do aerobics and run – isn't that enough?'
Comment: Aerobic exercise is great for cardiovascular fitness, but it won't make you strong or improve your metabolic rate. We have seen many marathon runners with trim legs, but flabby, underdeveloped upper body and arms.

'Lifting weights will make me look muscle-bound.'
Comment: All our celebrity clients train with weights to keep their great shape. Their muscle increases by about 20 per cent – enough to make an enormous difference in their metabolism and shape, but they become many sizes smaller, not larger! What they lose is all the extra fat padding that had been destroying their self-confidence and body image. The quality of a person's physique and health is in direct proportion to their commitment to exercise and nutrition.

'I'm tired and lethargic – I just don't have the energy.'
Comment: Poor energy levels can simply be a symptom of being overweight, having vitamin and mineral deficiencies and being unfit. Following the healthy-eating plan and exercise programme laid out in this book will dramatically increase your levels of performance and energy.

Before and after photos

It is vitally important to set up as many benchmarking tools as you can in order to maintain motivation and increase your chances of success. One of the best ways to do this is visually, by keeping a photographic record of what you looked like when you started, and what you look like after 8 weeks. And remember – the camera never lies!

One of the ways we have been conditioned to track our shape is on the scales. However they can only measure how much pressure your feet are placing on the earth – and nothing more! Scales can't tell you how much fat you're carrying, or how much your muscle tone is improving. They can't describe how your shape is changing, how many dress sizes you have come down by, how much straighter you are standing or how your cellulite is vanishing. A tape measure and bodyfat callipers can do a far better job in this respect, and can help calculate how much of your weight is fat, where it is coming off and how your shape is changing (see pages 40–41).

But these are all just numbers and the changes happen in very small steps. We know it's very difficult sometimes to keep motivated when you can't see from day to day how all these changes are taking place but you will be able to see the changes over a wider time frame by keeping a photographic record every month or two months. This will become another very useful weapon in your arsenal.

To get a totally honest view of yourself a photo in your bikini is best, as we often choose our favourite clothes for the way they camouflage our physique, or hold it in. If you have been hiding your physique away lately and have had no reason to wear a bikini, we suggest you go out and buy a cheap, plain dark-coloured one you can use for these first shots. For an accurate record, you should take one photo from the front, one from the back and one from the side.

Most of our clients are quite shocked when they see their pictures – especially the view from the back, as we hardly ever see ourselves from this angle. However, it is one of the best ones to take, and one that will show the most significant changes to your body shape.

This back view will show dramatic changes, such as how your shoulders are straightening, how the definition in your upper back is improving and how the cellulite on the back of your thighs is disappearing. You will also be able to see where the fat has vanished from your arms, the rolls around your bra strap and the side of your hips, and how your bottom line has lifted.

You'll see the changes to your size and silhouette from the side and front as well, this latter angle being best for observing how your face has become lighter (especially around the eyes), more defined and more youthful. Your photographs will also show how your skin texture has changed, smoothed out and started to glow again.

> ❛Scales can't tell you how much fat you're carrying, or how much your muscle tone is improving...but you will be able to see the changes over a wider time frame by keeping a photographic record.❜

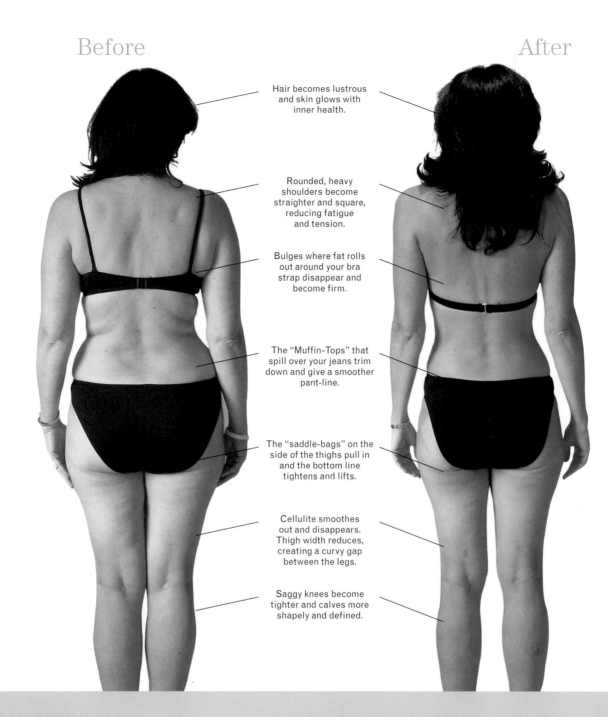

Before

After

Hair becomes lustrous and skin glows with inner health.

Rounded, heavy shoulders become straighter and square, reducing fatigue and tension.

Bulges where fat rolls out around your bra strap disappear and become firm.

The "Muffin-Tops" that spill over your jeans trim down and give a smoother pant-line.

The "saddle-bags" on the side of the thighs pull in and the bottom line tightens and lifts.

Cellulite smoothes out and disappears. Thigh width reduces, creating a curvy gap between the legs.

Saggy knees become tighter and calves more shapely and defined.

CLIENT A

43, graphic designer

This mother of three had a chronic back problem and had never lifted weights when she came to us. She lost 13.6 kg (30 lbs) and dropped 3 dress sizes on the Turn Back Your Age Clock programme .

She showed significant improvement after 8 weeks, including better posture and strength, and after 12 weeks her waist was down by 11 inches and she was wearing jeans she hadn't worn for years.

Help! The nuts and bolts are coming loose

Do you feel as strong and energetic as you used to?

Do you feel exhausted at the end of the day?

Is it increasingly difficult to maintain your weight?

Do you always catch seasonal flu and colds?

Do you forget where you've put down your keys?

It doesn't have to be this way! We were not born with an instructional manual nor taught how to programme ourselves for optimal health, so body care becomes driven by bad habits. Learn to question and challenge what it takes to operate this great machine and you will be rewarded with control over how you look and feel for life.

Get younger from the neck up

Before you can move on with the business of crafting a better body for longer, there are a number of points you must consider, accept and adopt into the ways you think and behave. Just take it one step at a time, get your head right and your body will follow.

Origin of the species

The human form is a highly evolved survival machine. Looking around at people, it's difficult to imagine that humans developed as efficient hunter-gatherer animals and, with the further development of our powers of reasoning, thought and consciousness, progressed to the top of the food chain. Our ability to do so was dependent on staying strong and fit, lean and hard. We hunted out, and were nourished on, fresh organic foods – meat, fish, root and leafy vegetables, fruits, berries, nuts, seeds and pure water. Whatever you see today in the mirror, underneath nothing has changed. We are still designed to run, lift, drag, dig, hunt, haul, climb, fight and even kill with our bare hands if necessary. No one was made to be out of shape, including you!

Compensate for modern living

Everywhere we look, there's another invention designed to make our busy lives easier. From the age of 25, our bodies start to fall apart from inactivity, toxicity and bad nutrition. We become gradually fatter, weaker, shorter, slower and dimmer. If you are to halt and even reverse these symptoms, there's no choice – you must prioritize some time to the requirements of your body every single day.

The age escalator

Maintaining our health against aging is like going down an escalator – the longer we stand in the same place, the further we get carried down, until we eventually reach the bottom. We need to turn around, face the other way and spend some

time and energy heading up in the other direction. Whatever your approach to health and aging, you're either walking up or you're walking down – there's no middle ground. Even to stay in the same relative position you have to walk up!

Put yourself first

In pursuit of getting everything done for other people (including employers), there's often little time to devote to ourselves, and as a result we end up frustrated, stressed, exhausted and confused. Our work suffers, our relationships break down and our bodies begin to fall apart at the seams. You need to break this cycle now. Your body is the most important thing you will ever possess – if it breaks down, you will not only become useless at the things other people have been relying on you for, but you will also be a burden to them. Look after yourself so that you can look after others.

Change your PDPs

Every decision we make is based on the system of experiences and beliefs that creates our Personal Default Positions (PDPs). These are the personal rules, values and policies that help us achieve satisfaction in our lives. Stepping outside these parameters is unusual, uncomfortable and normally very short-lived.

For example, it may be your default action to take the car to work each morning, even though it's only five miles from your home to the office. It becomes a habit and something you expect of yourself, and others expect too. If one sunny day you decide to ride your bicycle instead, this would be an unusual thing for you to do as a car driver, may well raise comment from your colleagues and will likely be a short-lived action. Sooner rather than later you will revert to driving the car again.

However, if one day you decide that in order to get more exercise into your day from now on you will become a cyclist instead of a car driver, your default position changes to habitually riding your bicycle to work every day. This doesn't prevent you from occasionally taking the car, perhaps in exceptionally bad weather, but to do so would be an unusual action for a habitual exerciser and cyclist, and would only be temporary or short-lived. Sooner rather than later you will revert to cycling again, enjoying the fitness and health benefits that it provides.

Likewise, many people have a Personal Default Position that allows them to have an alcoholic drink when they feel like it. Having a drink with a restaurant meal may be your PDP, but if you recognize that drinking alcohol is a very damaging habit, to both your health and your appearance, you might decide to change to only drinking alcohol on special occasions. This will protect you from its dependency, toxicity and aging effects without robbing you of the ability to enjoy it without guilt, when you choose.

These subtle changes in Personal Default Positions will alter the habitual actions that may have previously been holding you back from gaining the physique, energy and youthfulness you are now seeking. If you examine your current lifestyle choices, you will find that there are many other areas where your PDPs have been preventing you from improving your life, and from which you could benefit easily by changing.

Rejuvenator principles

Over the years we have incorporated many success strategies that have helped hundreds of people to transform and improve their physique in super-quick time. To turn back your body clock and rejuvenate your life, adopt these seven important principles of change.

1 See yourself as you are

We see ourselves so often that we become accustomed to what we see. The perception of our physique and what shape we are really in is often not 'in sync' with reality. Look closely and objectively in the mirror when you next step out of the shower and identify all the areas that need improvement, such as flabby arms, a bulging stomach or a double chin.

2 Become a student of your own body

Don't think that 'ignorance is bliss' and blindly follow the next new diet, as this will cause your body and your health to get out of shape. Seek out independent advice and research. Make an effort to go to seminars on cooking, or health-related topics that interest you, and keep increasing your knowledge about good nutrition and its effects. The more you know about the mechanics of your body, the easier it becomes to turn back your age clock.

3 Have a plan

Until today, you may have been living in your comfort zone, wishing your body was different, making a few changes but not putting any real effort into driving yourself to better health. Rather than just wishing for change and always looking for the next quick fix, you have to make a definite and binding decision to change both your mindset and your habits. Write down your goals and objectives, and then tell others about them, as you *must* honour these agreements.

Think about how you want to be in 10, 15, 20 years time. How will you look and how will you feel? Part of your plan must be to make time for yourself first. Your health, your vitality and your longevity will be the umbrella under which your family and others around you can flourish. Just living long is not good enough. Living well is the new challenge of our time.

4 Set goals

Meeting goals and managing your body with design and commitment will help you to look and feel great, but goals do need to be SMART:

- Specific ('I will take my lunch to work five days a week')
- Measurable ('I will keep a food log to check that it is happening')
- Achievable ('I will put aside an extra portion from dinner in a container for lunch the next day')
- Realistic ('The only extra cooking I have to do is 60 seconds in the microwave at work')
- Time-framed ('I will start this next Monday')

You need to know what is working and what is not working. Don't become one of those people who do exactly the same thing for months and never see any change. If you want different results, you must take a different approach.

5 Don't make excuses!

How many times do you say you would like to have a physique like a movie star or a friend, but shrug at the possibility because they have all the advantages – good genes, plenty of time, more money? These are all fallacies: some of the unhealthiest people are wealthy, some of the busiest are in the best shape and genes count for very little. What those people do have is motivation, commitment to change and control of their bodies.

6 Find motivation

No great feats were achieved while dwelling in our comfort zone. It is only through deadlines and pressures that we respond and grow. Many people have started off a new diet totally excited about the new regime that is finally going to get them into fantastic shape, but something goes wrong. Research shows that, when the going gets boring, people who are active and have sound, clear and measurable goals are much more successful than people who just take it easy. Any sort of competition is a powerful motivator for most people – to be a successful competitor, start with easily achievable goals. There'll always be setbacks, but persistent and successful achievers always get to their goal. Keep yourself motivated and updated – be interested in the latest research topics in fitness and health. Read up on articles written by athletes, scientists and independent health researchers.

7 Invest in the future

Your body is the only vehicle you have to take you through life, and yet people spend more money on cars, holidays and clothes than they do on their physiques. The decision you take now to improve and repair your body is a commitment and an invaluable investment in the future. You only have one body and it is the most important asset you will ever have. A great physique is the ultimate fashion statement and one that cannot be bought.

Are you truly living?

Experts now say that many people live quite well until they are 25 or so, after which they start to 'disintegrate'. Of the four stages of health below, living in Stages 1 and 2 is, unfortunately, the most common state of the majority of our population, and as a result our bodies are propped up on little else than medication and hope. Yet we know that anyone, at any age, can look better, feel better and think more clearly, so striving to advance up to the optimum level of health is a reality for us all, if we so choose.

FOUR STAGES OF HEALTH

Stage 1: Slowly drowning
(requires no effort)

- Sickness/headaches – bad diet, caffeine/alcohol damage, no exercise
- Chronic fatigue – poor sleep, dehydrated, vitamin/mineral deficiency
- Low threshold to bugs/flu and so on – collapsed immunity, heavy reliance on medication
- Difficulty making it through the day – low energy, poor resilience, lack of concentration
- Numerous days off – feelings of hopelessness, frustration, depression

Stage 2: Just keeping head above water
(requires some effort)

- Occasional sickness, risk of disease – struggling immunity, 'as required' medication
- Just enough, but no spare energy – eating better, but snacking for energy, sleeping OK
- Only just make it through the day – exercising occasionally, needing weekends to recover

Stage 3: Swimming strongly
(requires consistent, conscientious effort)

- Ability to get through the day without difficulty – more confident, clear-headed, positive
- Energy and fitness to pursue leisure activities – healthier and more balanced diet, sound sleep
- Maintaining healthy body shape/composition – exercising 2–3 times a week, body-conscious
- Few instances of illness/fatigue/aches/pains – no requirement for stimulants, sugar or drugs

Stage 4: Running on dry land
(requires discipline, commitment, smart thinking)

- High level of activity possible – strong, fit, dynamic, exercising hard most days
- Great body shape and composition – lean, toned, feeling sexy and supremely confident
- Boosted energy and mood levels – animated, alert, on top of game, optimal nutrition
- Instances of illness rare – immunity strong, risk of disease minimal
- High levels of enjoyment of life – ability to seek and triumph over new challenges

Stage 4 is excellent health and is attainable at any age. It requires consistent and mindful work to maintain, but the rewards are huge!

What really is fitness?

Fitness for optimal health consists of four essential interacting components that have equal importance. It's like a four-legged stool – all the legs must be the same length or it becomes unstable.

1 Aerobic fitness

This is the measure of the heart's ability to pump oxygen-rich blood around the body to organs and working muscles. An unfit heart is like an old car engine labouring under a heavy load, making you puff when you go upstairs or dash to catch a bus. A healthy, trained heart is like a high-powered new engine: it will pump greater volumes of blood around your body with each stroke, giving you increased energy. You can be aerobically fit but neither strong nor toned.

2 Muscle strength

The muscles of the body are like a corset keeping the internal organs firm and shapely, while providing support for the bones to give good posture. Muscle strength is vital to hold your bones in the correct position, keeping you free from imbalances that can lead to injury. Muscles play a vital role in weight loss, since they are greedy calorie burners. They also help to keep your hormones stable and stimulate the release of 'feel-good' endorphins. Muscle strength is not to be confused with muscular endurance, which is how long your muscles can work before becoming fatigued. You can be strong but not fit.

3 Flexibility

Functional flexibility of the muscles, ligaments and tendons around all your joints is vital for good posture, balance and mobility. Lack of flexibility in specific areas will leave the body prone to injury and pain, which gradually increases with age. Muscle tightness can also destroy your posture, creating a stooped, hunched or collapsed frame. You can be flexible but neither fit nor strong.

4 Nutrition

In order to improve performance, to get fitter or to lose fat, exercise works on an overload principle. This dictates that extra stress needs to be placed regularly on all the structures within the body for improvement, maintenance and repair of its functions. For this to happen successfully, we must fuel the body with superior levels of nutrition. Training long and hard while severely restricting food, or eating junk food, will not achieve the desired results.

The strong stay young

This is the number one secret to turning back your age clock. To look and feel your best, you must train with weights. Muscle is youth, shape, energy, vitality and virility – physical weakness robs men and women of their youth.

Modern automation has engineered many of the harder physical activities out of our daily lives. We can now sit on the sofa and answer the phone, open and shut anything we choose with a remote control and shop anywhere for anything without raising more than a finger. Our muscles and bones are only as strong as the current forces exerted upon them, because that is one of the processes of regeneration. Unfortunately, the body does not store fitness, and a healthy, athletic young man or woman can just as easily turn into a weak, middle-aged couch potato, with all the associated problems, as their sedentary counterparts. Blood pressure inflates, arteries become clogged, body fat balloons, strength wanes, balance teeters and intelligence vacates the premises!

Many adolescents have great muscle tone and shape because their physiques are still maturing, and a sedentary lifestyle or years of eating on the run hasn't caught up with them yet. You don't ever need to lose this strength and vigour if you can only understand the correct exercise required to maintain it.

Exercise – the 'anti-aging pill'

Studies have found that exercise is the closest existing thing to an 'anti-aging pill'. People who are physically fit, who eat a healthy, balanced diet and who take the right supplements can turn back their biological age clock by at least 20 years – that's two decades of extra time free from mental and physical disease and degeneration.

There's a common myth that a challenging exercise routine is not normal and only for the budding athlete or 'health nut', and that a walk in the park is all the average person needs to stay in great shape. Wrong! Dismissing hard physical fitness as the domain of athletes is the very thing that has led people to become overweight, sluggish and unhealthy, with all the accompanying emotional problems.

Because of our hunter-gatherer ancestry (see page 14), it is unnatural that we now challenge our bodies so little.

We were designed to be lean, fit and extremely physical in a difficult and sometimes hostile environment. The quantity of food was scarcer then, but the quality was three times more nutritious. Therefore, regular and challenging levels of physical stress invigorate rather than degenerate, and make us feel good, because that is what we were built for.

Benefits of exercise

There are many good reasons to strengthen your muscles and bones through regular exercise – the most important ones for turning back your age clock are described below.

Reduce muscle shrinkage Every decade from your 30s onwards, you are likely to lose 2.5–4.5 kg (5½–10 lb) of muscle. This may not be particularly noticeable, but your shape just doesn't look or feel as good as it used to – fat has replaced muscle. Muscle shrinks with disuse, and by the age of 60 it's possible you might have lost as much as 25 per cent of your calorie-burning machine. Muscle is your metabolic engine, and the less muscle you have, the more spare calories you'll have left over from every meal that will turn to fat! This surplus can add up to an unconscious ability to stash an extra 500 fat calories a day – a big difference when you're trying to lose weight.

Improve libido Muscle helps to balance hormone levels in both males and females, as women also produce testosterone, though in smaller quantities than men. The leaner and more toned you are, the more testosterone you will generate and the better your sexual health will be. At any age, muscle is the best natural method of increasing potency. Unfortunately, the myth that women shouldn't do heavy weight training has caused immense frustration to those trying to find a workable solution to their flagging sex drive. Keeping hormones balanced and testosterone levels in a healthy range are important factors in improving and maintaining the female sex drive.

Prevent diabetes As muscle mass shrinks, blood sugar levels can increase. High levels of blood sugar cause acid to eat into the connective tissues of our skin, joints, ligaments and bones – all very aging. Put simply, muscle is the primary place your body puts the sugar you eat; if you're active, that sugar is burned by muscle, with some kept in storage as reserve fuel. If you're sedentary, or eat too many refined foods, surplus sugar is converted straight into fat. As a person becomes fatter and slower with less muscle, insulin (the hormone that regulates blood sugar levels) doesn't work as well, and blood sugar acid rages through your system. This affects everything from skin and hormones to emotional well-being.

Prevent osteoporosis Shrinking, looking fragile and losing your posture is aging. Osteoporosis, a thinning of the bones, is now a threat to both sexes, and is the cause of 'dowager's hump'. Bones are constantly being renewed throughout our life in the exact response to the stress put on them by daily activity. We have constant weight-bearing through our hips and legs, so the bone and muscle shrinkage starts in the upper body and spine. The exercise circuits in this book will increase bone density more than just doing aerobic activities. The correct resistance exercise also stresses most major bones in the body, helping to strengthen, build and protect against osteoporosis.

Sculpt an enviable shape You can't spot-reduce fat from your body, but you can certainly sculpt your physique. We have taken many very overweight, unhealthy clients through to compete successfully in national natural physique contests. There is no better age remedy for the slouch-shouldered, bulging-bellied person approaching middle age than to start sculpting their body. Weightlifting gives you tremendous control over how you look and feel. Muscles get stronger, your posture straightens and the bulges go away. It's rare for those who train correctly to have cellulite, as it changes you from inside out. Clothes will sit well on your frame and you can buy for style instead of camouflage.

Stabilize joints Strong muscle protects and stabilizes your joints and prevents falls. This is essential for improving your sports performance, as well as for everyday tasks such as catching a bus, dodging traffic, pushing open heavy doors, unscrewing stiff jar lids, negotiating stairs, lifting a pot of hot water or carrying groceries. Weak muscles and joints will rob you of your independence.

Increase physical energy Constant tiredness will age you faster and drain your health. This condition is called sarcopenia ('sarco' means flesh or muscle and 'penia' means loss). For an example of how easily precious muscle can be lost, look at the size of an arm or leg after a plaster cast supporting a broken bone has been removed – the limb emerges almost withered. A weight-training programme to increase muscle strength will have a profound effect on your physical appearance, performance and health, by improving your metabolism, which in turn will keep your energy levels high all day long and fat from creeping around your middle!

Increase mental and emotional energy The increasingly common fallback of 'comfort eating' is better and more accurately described as 'emotional eating'. If you feel upset because you're fat, eating chocolate is not going to help. In fact it will only make you fatter, and therefore even more upset. Your body and mind are not separated at the neck – they are part of the same organism. Regular exercise and

better nutrition are clearly the best place to start. Then training specifically for strength produces a range of physical benefits that will release positive emotional energies. These include improved self-confidence, feelings of self-empowerment, success and stability in life, and happiness with the way you look and feel.

Improve cardio health and circulation Incorporating regular aerobic exercise (see pages 86–87) in your weekly routine will bring plenty of benefits to your cardiovascular system (heart, lungs and circulation). These include lower blood pressure, improved blood supply to all muscles, prevention of varicose veins, greater lung capacity and oxygen uptake through the lung capillaries, increased fitness and endurance of the heart muscle, lower cholesterol and improved cellular tone as blood supply is brought to the skin.

Improve hormone balance Levels of serotonin and dopamine, related to brain aging, are improved in adult people who include weight-bearing exercise in their routine. Similarly, levels of human growth hormone (HGH) are increased with this particular type of exercise, making it easier to keep body fat at bay and your metabolic rate high. Fit and active men maintain their testosterone levels and virility well into old age, whereas the unfit show lower testosterone levels at all ages – women as well need to protect their levels of this valuable hormone. Insulin and glucagon, the sugar-balancing hormones, are also thrown out of balance with a sedentary lifestyle.

Healthy, fit women have a much easier time through premenstrual and menopause stages; period pains, mood swings, hot flushes and anxiety are greatly reduced. Exercise also has a direct beneficial effect on the hormones of emotions and stress. Incidences of depression rise in women reaching perimenopause and thereafter, and also in men as they age. Regular, intense workouts produce feel-good chemicals in the brain called endorphins, and these stimulate positive emotions that influence the whole body.

Prevent injuries. Our body was designed to be active when not sleeping, but because most of us have a more sedentary work pattern, we have become prone to muscle imbalances causing chronic injuries and pain. By strengthening and stretching these weak muscles that are often immobilized in our daily routine, we can prevent and reduce ongoing injuries.

Know where you stand

We don't usually give our sense of balance much thought, but by the age of 35 it starts to decline and at the age of 60 it will start to affect our daily functions. Taking steps to preserve it can be instrumental in turning back our age clock. Great posture is another wonderful anti-aging tool: when our organs, bones and muscles are in ideal alignment, we move with ease, function well and stand tall.

Keeping the balance

Our sense of balance is finely programmed to keep us upright via three systems:

Vision This is extremely important for our balance. The balance exercise below seems easy when your eyes are open, but by closing them you have to rely on the next two internal sensory systems for stability.

Vestibular system Tiny receptors in the inner ear send messages to the brain to control head balance. You just have to experience dizziness to know the impact this can have on your upright position.

Proprioception A network of receptors reports to the brain from the muscles, joints and the skin throughout the body. You can tell if these are not working – try using a phone after your arm has 'gone to sleep'! These systems operate constantly, even in sleep. To be at their sharpest and to work longer, they need proper nutrition and the right exercise.

The good news! For our balancing reflexes to work effectively, our muscles must be strong and our joints supple. By constantly strengthening the muscle tissues, all the serving structures to those areas are invigorated. Any exercise is good, as long as it challenges your body with different positions, movements and actions.

BALANCE EXERCISE

Practise the following exercise twice daily with your eyes open (8–10 attempts if need be) until you can do it successfully. Then do it with your eyes closed. If you have difficulty performing the step patterns, stand on one leg and simply point the other leg out towards each clock position without landing on it.

Imagine yourself standing in the middle of a clock face, with 12 directly in front of you. Take one lunging step with your right foot out towards 12, put your foot down and hold the lunge position. Retreat, and then take a similar step slightly to the right towards 1.30, then far to the right at 3, then step back onto 4.30 and 6. Do the same with your left foot, working anticlockwise from 12 through to 6.

X

✔

- Stand in front of a full-length mirror and observe your posture from the front or side.
- Stand tall and stretch the crown (back) of your head up towards the ceiling, lengthening the neck.
- Check to see that your head is not craning forwards and your chin is tucked in and down.
- Roll your shoulders back and down from your ears.
- Lift your ribcage up and out to the front.
- Check that your pelvis is centred and is not tilted forwards or back.

Posture is important

In a healthy body (viewed from the side) the spine takes the shape of a gentle 'S'. The head, chest, pelvis and ankle should sit in a vertical line. Then all the muscles, joints and bones will be in their natural biomechanical position and not tightened, rotated, compressed or restricted by any movement.

Carrying too much weight causes a shift in postural alignment. Bones and muscles respond to many pressures as we move, and an overload of body fat in one area or another will put extra strain on ligaments, tendons, long bones, joints and muscles in other supportive areas. Bad posture creeps up on us over the years, until misalignment becomes the comfortable position and headaches, strains and fatigue the norm.

Besides dramatically improving appearance, regaining great posture allows our internal organs to operate more efficiently. Our digestion works better, our lungs can inflate more fully and our lymphatic and vascular systems flow more efficiently. The benefits are felt throughout the body.

TIPS

- If you work at a computer, change the screen saver to read 'Posture check' to remind you to straighten up until your old habits and slouches are gone.
- Take time out to do the target-toning programme (see pages 120–131) and stretches for the neck during the day.
- Make it a habit to take deep diaphragmatic breaths – this helps you open out your chest, and energizes the whole system.

Test your real age

It is important to start intervening in the aging process as early on as possible. We can't manage what we don't measure, so before you start taking steps to turn back your age clock, it is important to assess your current health and fitness status. Here are some simple biomarkers of aging to give you an indication of the damage that may have occurred so far and a method of keeping track of progress as things improve.

The 13 biomarker tests

If you have any doubts about your current state of health and fitness, take these tests to find out the stark truth. You must be scrupulously honest at this stage.

Remember, however, that it's possible there could be an underlying medical cause for any changes or apparent problems in your body, so always check with your doctor before starting any fitness programme.

Your scores

A rating system has been applied to each test to give you an idea of your biological age and a figure for comparison after eight weeks on the programme. The rating systems have been guided by health-risk factors and by various government and fitness organizations' recommended levels of ability and performance for healthy or unhealthy individuals.

Test	Page		Result now	Result after 8 weeks
1 Skin elasticity	29	Age:		
2 Balance	30	Age:		
3 Vision	31	Age:		
4 Reaction speed	32	Age:		
5 Strength	33	Age:		
6 Flexibility	34	Age:		
7 Memory	35	Age:		
8 Blood pressure	36	Age:		
9 Resting heart rate	36	Age:		
10 Working heart rate	37	Age:		
		Tests 1–10 average:		
11 Lung capacity	38	Life expectancy:		
12 Waist circumference	39	Life expectancy:		
13 Body fat	40	Life expectancy:		
		Tests 11–13 average:		
Hydration	40–41	*See chart pages 40–41*		
Shape measurements	41	*See chart page 41*		

Calculating your biological age

When you have completed all the tests and filled in your answers in the score boxes, you will have a good idea of how old your body really is in biological terms. It's not as simple as just taking an average, however. If you score very poorly on one test, this may indicate a serious problem that needs urgent redress. The following tests have been divided into two sections. The first section assesses your skills, abilities and the state of your body and gives you an age score. The second section consists of tests that give you an indication of your life expectancy, based on risk factors. These will improve as you follow the programme. You should also monitor your hydration and keep a record of your shape measurements.

1 Skin elasticity test

Loss of skin elasticity tends to become noticeable in your 30s when wrinkles start to appear. This is directly related to the underlying deterioration of skin proteins. The three major influences on the aging of the skin are the quality of your diet, external factors such as environmental damage and inherited internal triggers.

Method Pinch the skin on the back of your hand tightly for one minute, then let it go. Count the number of seconds it takes for your skin to return to normal, and then compare with the charts below.

Rate yourself

Women	Time in seconds	Age rating	Men	Time in seconds	Age rating
	1	30		1	30
	2	35		1.5	35
	3	40		2	40
	6	45		4	45
	8	50		6	50
	10	55		9	55
	16	60		14	60
	24	65		20	65
	35	70		30	70
	40	75		40	75

2 Balance test

Balance is closely related to memory and reaction speed. Loss of balance is an aging condition that sneaks up on us and seriously reduces our quality of life. It can also lead to accidents.

Method Simply raise one leg out to the front with your knee bent at a right angle. Your arms can be stretched out to the side to assist. Now close your eyes and see how long it takes before you have to either return your raised foot to the ground, to prevent falling over, or open your eyes. For accuracy, get someone else to time you. (Alternatively, if you are standing in a queue, stand with one foot in front of the other, heel to toe, close your eyes and see how long you can stay in that position.)

Rate yourself

Time in seconds	Age rating
More than 30	20
20–30	30
15–20	40
10–15	50
Less than 10	60

3 Vision test

Our eyes were designed for a hunter-gatherer lifestyle –
sharp and agile with good distance vision and quick focus.
Now our hunting and gathering is done at eye level along
the supermarket shelves! All muscles benefit from regular
use to prevent atrophy or decline – even the tiny muscles
around the eyes.

Method Take out contact lenses or remove your glasses
if you wear them. Slowly bring a newspaper towards your
eyes until the regular-size letters start to blur. Get someone
to measure the distance from your eye to the newspaper
at this point.

Rate yourself

Distance	Age rating
10 cm (4 in)	20
15 cm (6 in)	30
30 cm (1 ft)	40
60 cm (2 ft)	50
1 m (3 ft)	60

4 Reaction speed test

Your reaction time will fall sharply with aging, and is closely related to memory and balance. You should be aiming to test yourself in these three areas regularly, to monitor any changes and take appropriate action.

Method Ask another person to hold a 30 cm (12 in) ruler in front of you, either at the tip marked '30 cm' or at the one marked '12 inches', depending on which system you are using. Position your open hand 10 cm (4 in) underneath the bottom of the ruler, with your thumb and forefinger ready to snap shut on the ruler. Without warning, your accomplice lets go of the ruler. The aim is for you to grab the ruler before it slips through your grasp, without moving your hand from its position. If you catch it, check off the measurement where your thumb is.

Rate yourself

Distance	Age rating
Less than 10 cm (4 in)	20
15 cm (6 in)	25
20 cm (8 in)	30
25 cm (10 in)	35
30 cm (12 in) or miss	40

5 Strength test

Keeping your muscles strong is key to staying young and fit. Muscle is definitely not just for the 'meatheads' in the gym! Many an older person has been confined into care, not necessarily because they are sick, but just because they are weak and therefore unable to perform many simple everyday tasks.

Method Men should use the press-up position where the body is in a straight line and only the hands and toes touch the floor. Using strict technique, lower yourself down until there is a 90-degree angle at the elbows and the upper arms are parallel to the floor. Continue to perform as many repetitions as possible, then rate your upper-body strength level against age by consulting the chart. If you have someone to assist you, they can place their clenched fist upright on the floor and you must touch the upper part of your chest against the top of their fist to count each repetition.

Women have the option of using the 'bent-knee' version of this exercise. Following the same strict technique for the press-up (as above), count the number you can perform until failure. Find out how you rate from the chart. Alternatively, if you are able to perform full-length press-ups as described above, rate your performance accordingly.

Rate yourself

Number of press-ups	Age rating
Men full length / women from knees	
30+	22
20–29	35
10–19	45
5–9	55
0–5	65
Women full length	
20+	20
10–19	25
5–9	35
1–4	45
0	60

6 Flexibility test

Flexibility is vital for injury prevention, movement and great posture. Flexibility is the full range of movement you have within a joint, such as the shoulder, hip or knee. Good flexibility allows the joints to rotate easily without causing pain and stress on the tissues surrounding them.

Method You will need someone to help measure your results. Bring one arm up behind your back. Now raise your other arm above your head and drop it down behind you to touch the hands together behind your back. Repeat on the other side. Ask someone to measure the distance between your two middle fingers.

Rate yourself

Distance apart	Age rating
0 (touching)	20
2.5 cm (1 in)	25
5 cm (2 in)	35
7 cm (3 in)	40
10 cm (4 in)	45
12 cm (5 in)	50
15 cm (6 in)	60
18 cm (7 in) +	70

BE FLEXIBLE!

Good flexibility improves your joints' range of motion. For example, flexibility in the shoulder muscles allows you to turn and put your hand over the seat as you reverse your car, to stretch your legs out when running fast and to look behind you without turning your whole body. These are all movement restrictions we see in older people, but ones that can be prevented. It is important in everything we do, from good posture to sitting comfortably. Flexibility is also essential for injury prevention. Injury causes scar tissue that tightens and interferes with your muscle balance.

When you have been injured and are working on regaining flexibility, it is essential to get that normal range of movement back. We are all guilty of assuming we tighten up as we age and shrug it off if perhaps only one shoulder can move further than the other. Stiff muscles and joints are aging and not normal in an active and balanced physique at any age! You can't assume someone is flexible just because they can touch their toes – you must be evenly flexible all over.

Daily, we overload and strengthen some muscles while others weaken through lack of use. Having a good balance of flexibility improves posture and movement, and prevents pain. Walk like a panther! Supple, fluid and graceful movements are all an indication of a youthful and healthy body.

7 Memory test

Have you ever found yourself in a shop and wondered what on earth it was you came for? As we age, most of us go through periods of forgetfulness. The brain can only deal with a certain number of tasks at one time, and when you are under pressure, it reduces focus on the habitual rituals we perform each day in order to function. Exercising your memory can keep it in good shape, however.

Method Read out the letters in each box below in turn. As soon as you have done so, cover them up and on a separate piece of paper write down the ones you can remember, in the correct order. Then calculate your results as a percentage. For example, if you remembered 5 out of 8 letters, divide 5 by 8 = 0.625, then multiply by 100 = 62.5 per cent. At the end, add up all your percentages and divide the total by 6 to get an average. You can rate yourself overall by checking the chart below.

Letters	Number of letters	Number correct	Percentage correct
U M	2		
T Z L D	4		
I △ □ O # Z	6		
A V C Y I S E H	8		
L B F Q R P M A U X	10		
Z Q E C T B U M O N R V	12		

Rate yourself

Percentage correct	Age rating
100	20
90	30
80	40
70	50
60	60
50	70
40	80
30 or less	90

8 Blood pressure test

High blood pressure, or hypertension, damages the elasticity of the blood vessels and causes stiffening in the artery walls. Along with fatty plaque deposits, this makes it increasingly harder for the heart to pump blood around your body. Not only is this a major risk factor for a heart attack and stroke, but high blood pressure can damage the heart, kidneys and eyes. The heart pumps about 750 ml (1¼ pints) of blood through your brain every minute!

Your blood pressure level is found by measuring the force or pressure (in millimetres of mercury, or mmHg) of the blood against the walls of the blood vessels, and on their elasticity. The average ideal blood pressure is 120/80 mmHg (usually spoken as '120 over 80'), plus or minus 20 on each measurement. The first number represents the pressure in your arteries when your heart is forcing blood through them, and the second number the pressure in your arteries when your heart relaxes. Blood pressure varies during the day, so it's important to get more than one reading before assuming you have problems.

Method Get your blood pressure tested by a trained professional several times to make sure you have the correct reading.

Rate yourself Based on the second number in your reading (the diastolic number – the one that measures the pressure in your arteries when your heart relaxes), pick the reading that is closest to your own in the chart below.

Diastolic reading	Age rating
60–70	20
70–80	25
80–90	35
90–100	50
100 +	70

9 Resting heart rate test

A person's heart rate, or pulse, when at rest is a measure of how good your heart is at pumping blood around your body. If your metabolic state and whole system is balanced, you are operating at peak efficiency and this will be reflected in a lower resting heart rate. This state of health puts less pressure on your heart and blood vessels. The average heart beats about 60–80 times a minute when rested.

Method The best time to find out your true resting heart rate is in the morning, before you get out of bed. There are two ideal spots for taking your pulse: the radial arteries in each wrist, and the carotid artery, about 2.5 cm (1 in) on either side of your windpipe. Place your index and middle finger lightly over one of these arteries, count all the beats for 15 seconds, then multiply the count by 4 to get the rate for a minute.

Rate yourself

Beats per minute	Age rating
60	20
65	30
70	40
75	50
80+	60

10 Working heart rate test

You have already tested your resting heart rate (opposite), so now it's time to give your heart a workout. An easy indicator of cardiovascular function is the following step test you can do at home. If you become uncomfortable, or experience extreme shortness of breath, stop, note your time and heart rate and retest every month until you see an improvement.

Method Use a sturdy, firm step that's around 40 cm (16 in) in height. If you have a staircase in your house, usually the second step up from the floor or landing is about right. Follow this sequence:

1 Stand with your feet directly in front of the step, start timing and, with your right foot, begin to step up and down. The cycle is right foot up, left foot up, right foot down, left foot down. A complete movement should take around 3 seconds. Ensure your feet land securely on the step and you stand to your full height at the top.

2 After 1½ minutes, change to lead with the left leg (with no stopping). We all have a dominant side of the body, and leading with the opposite leg may feel awkward, but persevere – it is all part of getting your body balanced.

3 Immediately 3 minutes is up, stop stepping and count your heart rate for 15 seconds. Multiply this figure by 4 to give total beats per minute (BPM) and check this against the chart.

Rate yourself

Beats per minute	Age rating
Less than 110	20
110–120	25
121–130	35
131–140	45
141–150	55
151–160	65
Over 160	75+

11 Lung capacity test

We cannot exist without healthy lungs, and as oxygen cannot be stored for use later, this is the organ that is most likely to hasten our demise if not looked after. Exercise is imperative for healthy lungs to work at an intensity that makes you breathe deeply. Keep control of your weight, as fat building up around these vital organs and inside the abdominal cavity can restrict your air exchange.

Method A fit and functional person of any age should be able to do the following exercise. Light a candle and hold it out at arm's length. Take a deep breath and blow forcefully, extinguishing the flame in one breath.

Rate yourself

Result	Age rating
Blow out candle at first attempt	20
Fail to blow out candle at first attempt	60

12 Waist circumference test

Excess intra-abdominal fat is a disease risk and accelerates aging. There's an increased risk to a man's health if your waist measurement is more than 94 cm (37 in). For women, there's a risk of complications if your waist measures more than 82 cm (32 in). (These measurements apply to western European populations.)

Method With a tape measure, find the midpoint between the top of your hips and the lower border of the ribcage, and take a measurement around your waist.

Rate yourself

Measurement	Life expectancy
Women	
Under 71 cm (28 in)	100
71–75 cm (28–30 in)	80
75–80 cm (30–32 in)	70
80–85 cm (32–34 in)	60
85–90 cm (34–36 in)	50
Men	
Under 85 cm (34 in)	100
85–90 cm (34–36 in)	80
90–95 cm (36–38 in)	70
95–100 cm (38–40 in)	60
100–105 cm (40–42 in)	50

13 Body fat test

For good health, men should have around 15 per cent body fat and women 20 per cent. For optimal health and increased longevity, men should have 10–15 per cent, and women 15–20 per cent. Excess fat in your body just sits there, not burning calories but causing wear and tear on you.

Method The two best methods for home measurements of body fat are home caliper kits or a set of body composition scales, which measure your fat levels by running a low-voltage current through your body to detect the resistance fat creates in its path. These are accurate, and easy to use.

Rate yourself

Fat percentage	Rating	Life expectancy
Women		
12–17	Lean athletic	100
18–25	Healthy range	80
26–35	Overweight	65
Over 35	Obese	50
Men		
10–15	Lean athletic	100
16–20	Healthy range	80
21–30	Overweight	65
Over 30	Obese	50

Hydration

Dehydration makes your skin look wrinkly and your whole body requires plenty of water to function efficiently. Most people don't drink nearly enough non-alcoholic, non-sugary fluids, to keep themselves properly hydrated. Official recommendations are for an adult to drink 6–8 large glasses of water per day, and up to 1 litre (1¾ pints) of water per hour while exercising.

Method First thing in the morning, collect a urine sample in a clear jar, discarding the first part of the urine stream. Hold the jar in front of a white background and compare the colour of your urine to the chart below.

| 1 | 2 | 3 | 4 | 5 | 6 | 7 | 8 |

Shape measurements

This is not a test as such, but another way to monitor how your shape is changing. You need to know if your buttocks are lifting, if your knees are shaping up or if your thighs are getting toned.

Method Use a measuring tape to record circumferences of specific body sites, such as the upper arm, the chest (underneath the arms and over the most prominent point of the bust), the hips, the thighs, just above the knees and mid-calf. Measure in the same spot each time.

Track yourself

Body area	Measurement now	After 8 weeks
Upper arm		
Chest		
Waist		
Hips		
Bottom		
Upper thighs		
Above knees		
Mid-calf		

Rate yourself If your urine sample matches colours 1–3 you are well hydrated. If your urine sample matches a colour any higher up the scale, you need to readjust your fluid intake to increase hydration. You may find it interesting to compare your urine before and after exercise to show how much fluid is lost when you sweat.

The colours printed below should be used as a guide only. Certain medicines and vitamins may cause the colour of your urine to change. If any of these have been taken, this test is unreliable.

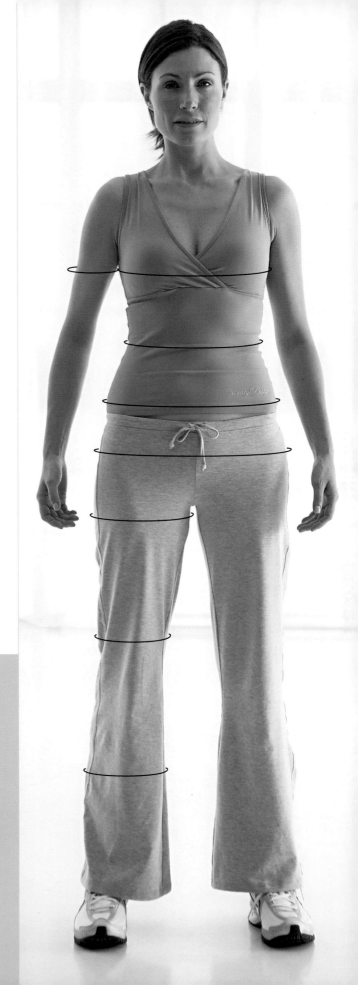

The master plan

Now that you have completed all the tests and discovered the truth about your biological age, it's time to start doing something about it. The eight-week master plan is designed to turn your life around, building up gradually in intensity so that you won't be tempted to give up, and if you stick to it you will see dramatic changes in both your physical shape and energy levels. Everyone – especially you – will be amazed at the transformation!

Before you start

Here's a quick reminder of the order in which you should be doing things if you want to turn back your age clock drastically in the space of eight weeks.

- Get a full medical from your doctor – it's a good idea to get their clearance before commencing on any new regime of exercise or nutrition.
- Take all the tests for aging biomarkers and rate yourself on the scores where provided.
- Read and reread the tips and hints we've supplied to help you through, especially in the diet and exercise chapters.
- Plan your meal schedule for the next three days (or even up to a week if you can), including everything you're going to be eating at every meal as best you can.
- Shop for all the ingredients you need for the next three days.
- Get set up with your exercise environment and equipment, if required. Set up a training log and nutrition log.
- Take all your measurements and a set of 'before' photos.
- Follow the eight-week master plan.
- Retest yourself on the aging biomarkers and retake your measurements at the end of the eight weeks.

Set a date now

There's never a magic time. Life will always be something of a rollercoaster and the most vital thing you can do is take control of your body **now**, to ensure you will always be in the best possible health to ride out the storms. The pay-off for perseverance is a younger, empowered, confident, healthier and happier you. Don't put it off – the sooner you start, the better!

Get prepared

The first thing to do is clear out all 'aging' foods (see page 69). Then go shopping and buy in plenty of the 'authorized' foods mentioned in the diet chapter (see the list of 'superfoods' on page 73) and become a 'student of your own body' (see page 48). Now have a look at the workout chapter and make a list of any items of equipment that you are going to need, such as a pedometer, dumbbells or stability ball (see pages 94–95). Go out and buy these items, or order them in, immediately.

Take some 'before' photos

This will feel embarrassing, but it gives you a chance to see yourself dispassionately, and to look at the areas that are not so bad and areas that may be hindering your progress. Photograph yourself from the front, side and back, dressed only in a bikini or swimming shorts. These pictures aren't for display, but they'll provide clear, documented proof as you go forward that you're changing – proof that the scales will not always show. This will be a powerful motivator!

Start a training and food diary

Use a small notebook and carry it with you at all times. Start by writing in your training sessions as fixed appointments. Try to keep a consistent time for your workouts (preferably morning).

For the first seven days, write down in your diary exactly **what** you eat (don't leave out condiments, for example), **when** you eat and **how much** you eat. Be as truthful as possible. Psychologists have found that we underestimate how much we eat and overestimate how much exercise we do, so write down immediately all the food you consume, as your recall won't be accurate and because so much food is eaten out of habit. At the end of each day, also record the type of exercise you have done, for how long you did it and the number of steps taken on your pedometer that day.

This diary will give you an insight into where your trouble spots may be, such as late-night eating, not enough food during the day or skipping exercise. As soon as you identify a problem, take steps to change things!

Week 1

Training plan

Day	Exercise	Duration
1	Bodyweight circuit (see pages 96–107)	• 20 seconds at each station • total circuit: at least 15 minutes
2	Aerobic activity of choice (see pages 86–87)	• at least 15 minutes
3	Bodyweight circuit	• 20 seconds at each station • total circuit: at least 15 minutes
4	Aerobic activity of choice	• at least 15 minutes
5	Bodyweight circuit	• 20 seconds at each station • total circuit: at least 15 minutes
6	Aerobic activity of choice	• at least 15 minutes
7	Day off exercise	

This week's tasks

Exercise This is the first week of the circuit, so start slowly and at your own pace. Don't rush – continue for 20 seconds. Pause for a breather if you need to. (If you're fitter, feel free to extend both the length of time at each station to 30 seconds, and the total duration of the circuit.) Remember to stretch after every workout.

Nutrition Start your food diary according to the instructions opposite, and keep filling it out as you go through the day for all of this week. Cut out any aging foods that you know won't be included in the programme. Start the day by having a substantial breakfast (see page 75 for ideas).

Lifestyle Write down your current weight and measurements, and also your body-fat measurements (because you are turning back your age clock in a healthy way, you need to know it's fat you're losing and not muscle). Record your ultimate goals for your body, being very specific – for example, 4.5–6 kg (10–14 lb) reduction in body fat, 8 cm (3 in) off the hips, losing 10–20 years in biological age.

TIP OF THE WEEK

Get a friend to do this programme with you – it's great motivational support, and you will spur each other on to do better!

Week 2

Training plan

Day	Exercise	Duration
1	Bodyweight circuit (see pages 96–107)	• 30 seconds at each station • total circuit: at least 25 minutes (if fitter, increase by 10 minutes to a max of 50 minutes)
2	Aerobic activity of choice (see pages 86–87)	• at least 25 minutes (if fitter, continue for up to 60 minutes)
3	Bodyweight circuit	• 30 seconds at each station • total circuit: at least 25 minutes
4	Aerobic activity of choice	• at least 25 minutes
5	Bodyweight circuit	• 30 seconds at each station • total circuit: at least 25 minutes
6	Aerobic activity of choice	• at least 25 minutes
7	Day off	

This week's tasks

Exercise Increase the time at each station and the total circuit duration by 10 seconds/minutes from last week. Identify one new CBO™ (calorie-burning opportunity™) you can do every day as part of increasing your general activity levels (see page 91). Make this a permanent rule.

Nutrition Pick two days from last week's food diary and compare each meal on each day to the model plate guidelines (see pages 74–75). Use the diagram to help you visualize how the meals should have appeared on your plate. Give yourself a percentage score as to how close you came to the ideal profile! Make sure you're having a broad-spectrum multivitamin with breakfast and high tea. Ensure there are no long gaps between your meals.

Lifestyle Start getting used to the idea that you are converting to a more generally active, youthful lifestyle. Wear your pedometer all day and aim to do at least 5,000 steps per day this week (your ultimate goal is 10,000 steps a day). Keep a running score of your vegetable intake and limit starchy carbohydrates after high tea (4.30 pm).

TIP OF THE WEEK

Make sure you are eating intentionally and not emotionally. Find a motivational picture of a physique you would like to achieve and pin it up where you can see it each day. Visualize yourself in that body.

Week 3

Training plan

Day	Exercise	Duration
1	Bodyweight circuit (see pages 96–107)	• 20 repetitions at each station • total circuit: 30 minutes
2	Aerobic activity of choice (see pages 86–87)	• 40 minutes
3	Bodyweight circuit	• 20 repetitions at each station • total circuit: 30 minutes
4	Aerobic activity of choice	• 40 minutes
5	Bodyweight circuit	• 20 repetitions at each station • total circuit: 30 minutes
6	Aerobic activity of choice	• 40 minutes
7	Day off	

This week's tasks

Exercise Change from doing 30 seconds at each station to doing 20 repetitions, regardless of how long it takes in each activity. Take the total duration of the circuit up to 30 minutes, but increase your aerobic activity by another 15 minutes to 40 minutes. Don't forget to stretch every day after every workout. Try to increase pedometer readings to 10,000 steps per day.

Nutrition Start working on preparing your meals in advance. Using a notebook as a meal planner, write in every meal you're going to eat over the next three days. Organize your shopping list from your planner, and aim to shop at least twice a week. Do a check on your storecupboards, fridge and freezer to ensure you have all the de-aging ingredients you need for your meals.

Lifestyle On Day 1, retake your measurements and check your exercise performance tests to see how you are progressing. Look for and become aware of the changes that are happening to your body – vibrant skin, toning of your arms, tightening of your abdomen. Congratulate yourself with a night out, a facial, a wonderful piece of clothing – anything you enjoy except alcohol (it's disruptive to fat loss and causes premature aging).

TIP OF THE WEEK
Tell everyone you know that you are embarking on this programme to change your lifestyle. They can encourage and support you along the way. Some people may feel uncomfortable with you changing for the better, so don't let saboteurs knock your confidence.

Week 4

Training plan

Day	Exercise	Duration
1	Bodyweight circuit (see pages 96–107)	• 20 repetitions at each station • total circuit: 40 minutes
2	Aerobic activity of choice (see pages 86–87)	• 50 minutes
3	Bodyweight circuit	• 20 repetitions at each station • total circuit: 40 minutes
4	Aerobic activity of choice	• 50 minutes
5	Bodyweight circuit	• 20 repetitions at each station • total circuit: 40 minutes
6	Aerobic activity of choice	• 50 minutes
7	Day off	

This week's tasks

Exercise Maintain doing 20 repetitions of each exercise, but now increase the total time of the circuit to 40 minutes. Duration of aerobic activities can also be extended by another 10 minutes to 50 minutes. By now, you should be making a de-aging rule to achieve a total of not less than 10,000 steps a day on your pedometer (remember that this includes your exercise sessions).

Nutrition As your natural metabolism will be increasing, use this week to cut out all stimulant drinks: coffee, energy drinks, black tea and so on. 'Age-proof' your kitchen against all staples that will entice you back to your old eating habits (see page 69). Try making meal preparation easier by cooking extra in the evening. Put aside two portions in containers, which will be your meals for lunch and high tea the following day. Ensure you are not aging your body by eating large meals late in the evening.

Lifestyle Keep researching this topic by subscribing to quality health and fitness magazines as part of becoming a student of your own body. Explore recognized nutrition websites and subscribe to their newsletters. Always look at the condition the person is in who gives you health advice. Remember – it is easier to eat to nourish your body and create time for a workout than it is to look in the mirror each morning and not like what you see or how you feel.

TIP OF THE WEEK
When on holiday, plan your activities around exercise and good food. You are never on holiday from your body!

Week 5

Training plan

Day	Exercise	Duration
1	Weights circuit (see pages 108–119)	• 30 seconds at each station • total circuit: 20 minutes
2	Aerobic activity of choice (see pages 86–87)	• 50 minutes • try to improve your distances/times
3	Target-toning programme (see pages 120–131)	• As instructed
4	Aerobic activity of choice	• 50 minutes • try to improve your distances/times
5	Weights circuit	• 30 seconds at each station • total circuit: 20 minutes
6	Aerobic activity of choice	• 50 minutes • try to improve your distances/times
7	Day off	

This week's tasks

Exercise This week there's a new circuit-format training with weights. Start off just doing 30 seconds of however many repetitions you're comfortable doing, and drop the circuit time back to 20 minutes to start with until you're comfortable increasing the duration. Maintain aerobic times, but try to increase the pace and/or distance you cover in the session. On Day 3, introduce the target-toning programme. Do each exercise completely before moving on to the next activity, rather than as a circuit.

Nutrition Your new nutrition mission this week is to create two new recipes you haven't tried before, ensuring the meal as a whole conforms to the model plate guidelines (see pages 74–75). Keep the ones you love and ditch the ones you hate,

and over the next few months you'll end up with a lifetime's worth of variety meals. Start another food diary alongside your planner and see how close it actually ends up!

Lifestyle Revisit your measurements and physical performance tests to monitor your progress! Sometimes we get so busy running around after others that we forget to exercise and eat when we should. Looking after your health is the most important thing you can do for yourself and for others, so always prioritize these things over and above any other obligations you take on.

TIP OF THE WEEK
Really work out as hard as you can now. The good news is that, if you work intensely, most negative moods and feelings of fatigue will quickly disappear.

Week 6

Training plan

Day	Exercise	Duration
1	Weights circuit (see pages 108–119)	• 30 seconds at each station • total circuit: 30 minutes
2	Aerobic activity of choice (see pages 86–87)	• 50 minutes • try to improve your distances and times
3	Target-toning programme (see pages 120–131)	• As instructed
4	Aerobic activity of choice	• 50 minutes • try to improve your distances and times
5	Weights circuit	• 30 seconds at each station • total circuit: 30 minutes
6	Aerobic activity of choice	• 50 minutes • try to improve your distances and times
7	Day off	

This week's tasks

Exercise Now you're more confident with the weights exercises, increase the duration of the circuit to 30 minutes, or if you're much fitter a maximum of 45 minutes. At each station with the weights, increase the level of resistance by one level (such as 1 kg/2 lb). Continue to up the pace of your aerobic activities, as long as you can sustain the exercise for up to 50 minutes straight. Try adding a recreational activity on your day off (walk, swim, cycle, play tennis).

Nutrition Check again and see how close you're getting to having a total of nine cups of anti-aging vegetables per day, spread over your main meals (see pages 72–73). See if you can munch on half of your vegetables raw – excellent for health and for face fitness! When booking into a restaurant for a meal, try ringing ahead to organize your preferences. That way you get what you need, you're respectful of the workload of the chefs and there's no fuss and bother trying to order while the rest of the table is waiting for you!

Lifestyle Maintain the practice of planning your meals three days in advance. Always do this, and dovetail it in with your work/social diary so that you always know what you'll be eating wherever you are at meal times. People who fail to do this consistently fail to maintain the physique they want. Set your stopwatch for small meal breaks, or make appointments in your computer so that it will remind you.

TIP OF THE WEEK

Plan always to have emergency food on hand wherever you are: protein bars, crudités, fruit and so forth.

Week 7

Training plan

Day	Exercise	Duration
1	Weights circuit (see pages 108–119)	• 20 repetitions at each station • total circuit: 30 minutes
2	Aerobic activity of choice (see pages 86–87)	• 50 minutes
3	Target-toning programme (see pages 120–131)	• As instructed
4	Aerobic activity of choice	• 50 minutes
5	Weights circuit	• 20 repetitions at each station • total circuit: 30 minutes
6	Aerobic activity of choice	• 50 minutes
7	Day off	

This week's tasks

Exercise Switch from doing 30 seconds at each station to completing 20 repetitions. Maintain total circuit length at 30 minutes. On target-toning day, increase your weights by one level (such as 1 kg/2 lb). Try something different for your aerobic activity – use a different machine, or if walking try a slow jog after every second lamp post!

Nutrition Try 'leaning out' your nutrition a little bit more – for example, poach your chicken or beef mince before grilling. Don't add unnecessary oil or butter to anything you cook or eat. Try to ensure most of your fresh foods are organic, and avoid any foods wrapped in clingfilm or soft plastic. Add in more raw vegetables now. When we heat food above 43° C (109°F), we damage important enzymes.

Lifestyle At the start of this week, retake your measurements and physical tests. Be patient and proud of the changes you have made. Reassure yourself that body fat takes less time to take off than it does to creep on. When ordering at a restaurant, eliminate the items that are obviously going to be loaded in fats and sugars. Ask if a pan-fried fish fillet could be steamed or grilled instead, or whether the steak can have the peppercorn sauce on the side or the vegetables can be served steamed without butter or sauces. Be assertive about your needs.

TIP OF THE WEEK

Plateaus can happen because of food or exercise complacency. The rejuvenator circuit is excellent for fat burning and for keeping your body on edge, but remember that you must work intensely.

Week 8

Training plan

Day	Exercise	Duration
1	Weights circuit (see pages 108–119)	• 20 repetitions at each station • total circuit: 45 minutes
2	Aerobic activity of choice (see pages 86–87)	• 50 minutes
3	Target-toning programme (see pages 120–131)	• As instructed
4	Aerobic activity of choice	• 50 minutes
5	Weights circuit	• 20 repetitions at each station • total circuit: 45 minutes
6	Aerobic activity of choice	• 50 minutes
7	Day off	

This week's tasks

Exercise Increase the duration of the circuit to 45 minutes, maintaining 20 repetitions of each exercise. Use your new fitness levels to explore a new sport or activity, such as tennis or climbing. After Day 7, take three days off exercise as a detraining strategy; then start back into the bodyweight circuit, doing up to 20–30 repetitions at each station for 45 minutes.

Nutrition Now your eating regime is optimal, continue to maintain the new habits you have adopted. Concentrate on learning to like new foods and how they make you feel. Old habits and tastes die hard, so be vigilant to avoid falling into old, aging behaviour patterns. Question the quality of the food you eat, know where it comes from and ask: 'Will this make me look better or worse naked?'

Lifestyle At the end of this week, do a final retest of all your measurements. Calculate the changes in your ratings in every test, write them into the chart and compare them with your original results. Take some 'after' photos and compare them with your 'before' ones. Congratulations – you can celebrate now you have wisdom and control, but don't break your routine. Just as you would not break a promise to a friend, you must never break the promise you made to yourself to de-age your body, get to your goal weight ... and stay there.

TIP OF THE WEEK
Now that you have achieved this increased fitness, challenge yourself to another goal. Run a mini-marathon, enter a body-shaping competition or do a cross-country run for charity. Keep the challenges going!

Your challenge completed

Your 'after' photos are looking fantastic and years have been stripped away. You will be a different person – changed from the inside out. What used to feel normal will be replaced by new eating and exercise patterns, new energy, a different looking body and a new understanding of what makes you tick.

Now that you are up to maintenance level, maintain these good habits, as they take time to establish, and beware the old, destructive ones waiting to take you unawares through this process. When you look and feel fantastic, remind yourself how hard you have worked and how toned your physique now appears and feels, so don't undermine your commitment to yourself to keep feeling younger and healthier.

If ever your clothes begin to feel tight again, never give in to the next size up. Success comes with taking control of your eating, and understanding how and what feeds the body and why it needs exercise to stay young.

This is your one and only body for this lifetime, so you might as well have one that looks great and performs wonderfully. Don't believe that your health, your weight or your aging is down to random luck. You hold the power to turn back your age clock because you choose the right attitude and the right behaviour to generate amazing results.

By implementing these key points, you can make a huge difference to how you age. Be positive, and keep challenging yourself. Maintain a happy outlook on life. Think young! We hasten our age clock if we spend too much time being unhappy, anxious, negative or pessimistic. Studies have shown that a good mental attitude is imperative to aging well. Staying optimistic and positive and knowing that life is a self-fulfilling prophecy is a key strategy. Like the body, if we take responsibility for our own thoughts, mental alertness and happiness, we can stay healthier and younger for longer.

Super skin

Many of us do not realize that our skin is affected more by what we put into our bodies than what we put on to them. It is perhaps our bodies' most apparent sign of aging, but there is no need to resort to expensive treatments or time-consuming beauty regimes to keep your skin looking young and healthy; eating well, staying hydrated and getting plenty of sleep are three of the main ways to improve and maintain the appearance of our skin.

Skin is your outer garment

Your skin is the largest organ of your body, serving as a protective barrier against the elements and environment. Waterproofing, bacteria-resisting and self-repairing, it helps you maintain a constant body temperature and assists in eliminating toxins from your body.

Although inner turmoil and external environmental assaults all conspire to change this amazing tissue, it's worth remembering that it's made up entirely of what you eat and drink. Skin cells grow from the inside out – they are constantly dying on the outside and being replaced from beneath. How they replicate themselves is directly related to the quality of what you put in your mouth.

It's within your power not only to live longer but also to look younger. We know through current research that lifestyle choices have a huge impact on your health, how you look and feel and the condition of your skin. Start thinking about your body and protecting your skin as early as you possibly can.

How skin ages

The face, like the body, has an 'age triangle' – wide eyes, full cheeks and glowing skin down to full lips and a narrow chin. Aging changes this triangle when the fat, muscle and connective tissue in the cheek area slackens with time and moves downwards, forming fine lines between the nose and mouth and hollows around the eyes and mouth. Jowls become more apparent, widening the chin and forming a noticeably heavier look as we develop expression lines, and the triangle is lost.

From the age of 30, changes start to occur in the nature of the skin and body as fewer human growth hormones (HGH) are secreted. There's a considerable decrease in the number of vitamins directed to the skin, and if your diet is short in basic vitamins, the skin starts to age more rapidly. The skin cells die faster than the body can produce new ones and the quality and quantity of connective tissue is reduced. Fine lines also start to form in places on the skin where there's constant and repetitive movement, such as around or in between the eyes.

From the age of 40, the rate at which your skin discards dead cells slows down dramatically and it can look dull and tired. Areas of skin losing elasticity will become more noticeable, as the loss of collagen and elastin, as well as declining levels of the hormones oestrogen and progesterone in women, result in deeper wrinkles and loss of moisture and vitality in the skin texture.

From the age of 50, the onset of the menopause in women, and the andropause in men, causes normal hormonal secretions to drop away. Skin becomes much thinner and less elastic, and there can also be a decrease in oil-gland activity. The face can suffer from bone and muscle loss, causing a decrease in its structural support. Blotches and age spots may become more prominent.

External skin treatments and cosmetic surgery

Treating aging skin is now big business, and applying various substances to its external surfaces can help repair dry, broken or blemished areas (see pages 58–62), but remember that you can basically only cleanse, scrub and protect your skin from the outside. It's also becoming almost commonplace for people to alter the appearance of their skin, especially around the face, through treatments such as chemical peels, dermal fillers, dermabrasion, muscle relaxants, lasers, botox or collagen injections and full or partial face-lift surgery.

These are last-resort solutions to be considered only after you have taken time to research thoroughly about the positive and negative effects of the various procedures, and have seen real examples and testimonials of the consulting surgeon. Aside from the potential risks involved, you shouldn't need to resort to expensive treatments anyway. Follow our advice and your skin will naturally rejuvenate from the inside out!

Improve your skin condition now

On the following pages, you'll find lots of advice about basic skin care that won't cost you the earth. Start right now, and your skin will be rejuvenated before you know it!

Try to relax Positive stress is healthy for the body, but negative stress increases free radicals and corrodes your health. Chill out – have you ever noticed how well your skin glows after a relaxing holiday?

Improve your diet Diet can play an important role in all skin conditions, helping to combat not just wrinkles and lines but other skin problems as well, including acne, dry or oily skin, eczema and psoriasis. Poor eating habits diminish the supporting muscle structures of the body and the face, causing the skin to sag because of the reduced supply of nutrients and antioxidants to the skin. Internal imbalance will always be revealed on the face. Eliminate processed foods and reduce alcohol intake, and increase whole foods and therefore fibre intake. Consume 8–9 different servings of fresh organic vegetables, 2–3 pieces of organic fruit and some organic lean protein every day. (See the diet chapter for more information and advice.) For a wonderful skin rejuvenator, nutrient boost and a great detox, try drinking freshly juiced or blended vegetables on ice each morning.

Damage limitation

There are many things you can do straight away to limit the damage to your skin that is inflicted by modern living every day:

Take care of your skin in the sun Vitamin D stimulated by the sun is critical to good health, but sunbathing during the hottest part of the day isn't. Apply a vitamin C cream under your sunscreen, and a wear a hat with a wide brim. This also shades your eyes and helps prevent squinting – a fast way to create 'crow's-feet' wrinkles around the eyes!

Be aware of pollution Living in a city and being surrounded by polluted atmosphere, land and water is aging for the skin, since airborne pollution is as damaging to our cardiovascular system as smoking cigarettes daily.

Increase your water intake Alcohol and anything containing caffeine, salt or sugar will dehydrate your skin cells, leaving them leathery, scaly or crêpey. Water plays a vital role in nearly all of our biological processes, from keeping us alert to lubricating our joints and maintaining a plump, youthful skin. Drink filtered water wherever you can.

QUIT SMOKING NOW!

Puckering of the lips creates extra wrinkles, and the thousands of toxic chemicals in cigarette smoke produce free radicals that damage a healthy skin (did you know even sugar has found its way into cigarettes?). The skin takes on a greyish hue as the small capillaries become starved of oxygen. Smoking will affect the colour, elasticity and general health of your skin, but here are some other pressing reasons to give it up as soon as you can:

- increased risk of heart disease, stroke, emphysema and lung diseases, including cancer
- shortness of breath and inability to exercise
- reduced fertility and risk to your unborn baby during pregnancy
- low energy and concentration levels
- impaired sense of taste and smell
- negative impact on non-smokers around you

For advice on how to give up if you're finding it really difficult, consult your doctor.

Take more exercise Exercise is excellent for skin health – the extra intake of oxygen carries nutrients to the skin, bolstering cellular rejuvenation, and the working muscles improve lymphatic function in removing waste and banishing cellulite (see page 64). Exercisers look younger, and have better skin and fewer wrinkles, than non-exercisers.

Keep a steady weight Gaining or losing small amounts of weight can create fine wrinkles through the constant stretching and tightening of the skin.

Take the right supplements Choose a high-quality organic linseed oil (omega-3), a multivitamin/mineral combination and antioxidant formula as a supplement to your diet for good skin and overall health.

Establish a good sleep pattern This is vital for healthy collagen and elastin production. Night is repair and maintenance time for your tissues, but it's a process that kicks in later in the sleep cycle, so getting 7–8 hours' sleep is ideal.

Get your hormone levels checked Falling oestrogen levels can thin the skin and decrease elasticity, so consult a specialized anti-aging physician who can perform this check for you.

Keep an eye out for changes If there is a significant change anywhere on your skin – such as a growing mole, a lump or large peeling layers – that you can't account for, you must see your doctor as soon as possible.

Basic skin care

Your skin is the external barometer of your health. When you are exercising properly and your nutrient intake is high, your blood sugar and insulin levels will be balanced, the toxicity in your system will be low, your skin will glow and you will look refreshed. But there are other things you can do to improve the appearance of your skin while you are waiting for results from the eight-week programme. Adopting a good cleansing regime and using only beneficial products are both essential. Good skin care from both inside and out will help protect your body and delay the aging process.

Skin-cleansing routine

Cleansing is an essential part of caring for your skin, to remove sweat, dead cells, make-up, street filth and impurities. Never drag the skin and always remember to remove make-up at night, however tired you are. Be consistent and regular with your routine. The key is to treat your skin gently with cleansing, exfoliation (when needed) and regular moisturizing and protection. There are many conflicting views on the use of toners and exfoliants among professionals, so go with what works best for you.

- Read the labels of any products you intend to use, in order to avoid irritating additives (see below). If your skin is sensitive, avoid products containing perfumes or colourants.
- Remove all make-up carefully. Use a soft cloth or cotton wool pads and a good-quality eye make-up remover to avoid damaging the delicate tissue around your eyes.
- Take a quick but thorough shower. Avoid very hot water and long showers or baths, as these can dry the skin.
- Use a mild soap with oils and emollients added (read the ingredients on the packaging carefully). Avoid strong soaps that strip the natural oils from your skin.
- If you have to use a defoliant, use a non-abrasive one, to smooth the skin's surface.
- The skin around the eyes is the first to show signs of aging. Use a fine cream in this area, patting it gently around the orbital bone with your finger, from the outside in.
- A good way to test if you need a body moisturizer is to wait 20 minutes after a shower. If your skin feels tight, you should apply a moisturizer. If your skin is very dry, you may want to apply it while your skin is still moist.
- After washing or bathing in the evening, gently pat or blot your skin dry with a towel and immediately apply a rich cream or night moisturizer to trap some of the moisture in the skin. Pat it gently into the skin in upward movements.

It is just as important for men to take good care of their skin to prevent the leathering and wrinkling that will age them prematurely. Shaving exfoliates the skin in a severe manner and leaves it exposed and vulnerable. An organic, nutrient-rich moisturizer applied sparingly will soothe and nourish the skin, and acts as a barrier against the elements. In the evening, men should cleanse, then apply an overnight cream or balm.

Anti-aging creams

Often manufacturers' claims regarding anti-aging creams are based on little or no scientific evidence. Depending on your skin type and age, consult a dermatologist or anti-aging doctor for specifically prescribed rejuvenating creams. Here are some proven topical anti-aging creams that could help you turn back your skin age clock:

- Alpha-hydroxy acids (AHAs, or 'fruit acids') and beta-hydroxy acids (BHAs, derived from willow bark) improve the skin's appearance by speeding up the shedding of old, dead cells from the skin surface. The down side is that they can irritate the skin, although BHAs are less irritating.
- Retinoid creams (prescription only) help the skin produce new cells more quickly. They are excellent skin rejuvenators, but they can also cause skin irritation.
- Vitamin A, C and E creams have a protective and antioxidant effect on the skin, and can help to boost circulation and collagen production.

Beauty products and their dangers

As far as external creams and lotions go, remember that the beauty industry is a multi-million dollar one designed to take your money, and it's difficult to know what to believe and which product – if any – to choose. If you have your sleep, diet and exercise correct, then your skin will look vibrant and healthy and your choices will not be so arduous. Always use organic or low-chemical products, which are made using only natural ingredients, selected for their non-toxic properties (although not all natural ingredients are non-toxic).

Being the body's largest organ, it is estimated that up to 60 per cent of what you put on your skin can end up in your bloodstream. Any chemicals are then transported to your liver, which attempts to remove them from circulation to prevent a build-up of toxicity in the blood. To keep healthy, glowing skin as you age, it's really important to be aware of what is in the skin-care product you use. Here are the ingredients to avoid:

- **Methyl paraben** is a common preservative that gives a greater shelf life. This and its derivatives, propyl, butyl and ethyl paraben, can trigger irritations on sensitive skins.
- **Propylene glycol** is used to provide texture and stability – it's the same chemical that's found in brake fluid and antifreeze.
- **Sodium lauryl sulphate** is a detergent and emulsifier found in many shampoos. It strips the skin of its natural oils, allowing better delivery of other chemicals, and has been linked to skin irritation, hair loss, dandruff and allergic reactions.
- **Synthetic fragrances** are highly allergenic. They are used in perfumes and many other scented products. Unfortunately, they are unregulated and unlisted, as well as mostly being toxic.

See the light

Light does matter. As well as making you feel great, the sun brings vital health benefits to the body and to your skin. Strike a balance, though, as over-exposure can damage and age your skin. Sunblock creams such as zinc oxide or titanium dioxide are the most powerful. Use clothing to cover up when necessary, as sunscreens made from chemicals can get absorbed through the skin and contribute to the body's toxic overload. If you have to use sunscreen, apply a pure antioxidant cream underneath first.

Your skin needs exercise!

Aerobic exercise boosts the circulation and takes oxygen-rich blood to every cell in the body, allowing nutrients to be absorbed and aiding new cells in the elimination of impurities and toxins. Keep your bones and muscles young and supple by training hard with weights, to protect your bone density and muscle shape – these are the supportive undergarments for your skin. Strength training helps detoxify the body by moving lymph along (see page 64) and improves the shape of the underlying muscle that helps gives skin its anchor. Like a good foundation garment, muscle can keep areas firm that are prone to sagging and wrinkling, such as the neck, cleavage, upper arms, inner thighs, buttocks, knees and abdomen.

SKIN CREAM RECIPE

Gotu kola (*Centella asiatica*) has proven effective in strengthening collagen. Buy a standardized extract containing 40 per cent asiaticoside. Mix with cocoa butter or jojoba butter – these are the best emollients, as they can help protect chemical changes that rob collagen of its solubility and flexibility. They also soften skin and enhance its flexibility. Mix the two together and you have a potent anti-aging, wrinkle-fighting cream!

Look after your lymph!

Lymph is a clear fluid that circulates throughout the body to cleanse tissues, keeping them free from toxic build-up, bacteria and other waste, leaving the skin radiant and the body healthy. The waste is filtered at various lymph node 'stations' around the body. It relies totally on the movement and power of your muscles – it has no propulsion system of its own. If you allow your lymph flow to slow or stagnate, then the dreaded cellulite is one of the possible results! A combination of good diet, proper exercise and the occasional massage will keep your lymph flowing freely.

BANISH CELLULITE

Cellulite is a substance commonly found on the hips, thighs and buttocks in women, but increasingly also on men around the waist and back of the hips. Our fat cells are held in hammocks of elastic and connective tissue, and serviced by our blood and lymph systems. As we age, the fat connective tissue gets weaker and the chambers of fat less supported; as they grow and become fuller and harder, the fat cells start to crowd out the lymph vessels. This leads to sluggish or even static regions of blood and lymph flow, and a consequent build-up of toxins. Eventually, the areas of greatest fat accumulation become visibly dense, lumpy and sometimes cold to the touch.

'Cellulite-busting' is big business, but cellulite is only damaged fat – there's just a lot of it where you see it, and you can banish it through improved diet and the right exercise, such as the circuits in this book. Don't expect it to disappear overnight, but do expect it to disappear.

Applying moisturizer (optional)

For a manual face lift, you can moisturize your skin (using very little cream) at the same time to help stimulate circulation. This is great for congested skin after an over-indulgent weekend, or for a perk-up from a stressful week. It is also wonderful when performed on a partner or friend.

1 Take a tiny bit of moisturizer, warm it between your fingers and pat gently on to the skin of your face, neck and chest.
2 Start low and massage your cream in an upward movement from the cleavage, smoothly gliding up to under the chin, one palm continually following the other very gently.
3 Repeat, spreading the cream along the jaw line to the ears and across the cheeks, sweeping outwards.

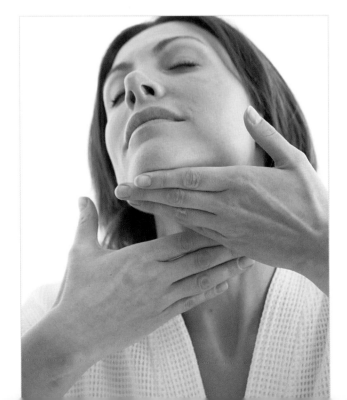

Rejuvenating lymphatic massage

There are approximately 160 lymph nodes around the face and neck. In the following massage, mild pressure movements are used on the walls of lymph collectors in this area. This helps to relieve puffiness, congestion and dark cirles around the eyes. It also stimulates and strengthens skin cells.

1 Place your middle and ring fingers, behind your ear lobe on each side of your neck. Gently press and move the skin in a semicircular movement to the count of three, then release. Do not drag your fingers over your skin – move the skin itself. Repeat this movement, slowly working your way down the side of your neck until you reach the clavicle (collarbone). Repeat three times, starting again from behind your ear.

2 Bring two fingers of each hand to the centre of the chin and repeat the semicircular press-and-release movement for the count of three. Work along the jaw line towards the ears. Repeat three times.

3 Place the middle and ring finger directly under your nose. Using the semicircular press-and-release movement, work your fingers away from your nose across your cheeks until you reach your ear lobe. Repeat three times.

4 Sweeping the fingers up the side of the nose, press and hold your ring finger on the inside corner of your eyes directly below the inner brow. Press and release four times.

5 Working along the eyebrow from the nose to the temples, use your index finger and thumb to squeeze your eyebrow gently to the count of three. At the outer edge of the eyebrow, move your fingers to the bone below the eye and repeat the movement, working your way back up to the inside of the eyebrow. Repeat three to five times, as there is often a lot of tension in this area.

6 Cupping the hands slightly, stroke up the forehead into the hairline in a continuous movement. Repeat eight times.

7 Move your ring and middle finger on to the temples, and with gentle semicircular press-and-release movements, massage at the outer edge of the eyes. Repeat three to five times.

8 Massage the ears between your thumbs and index fingers, starting at the ear lobe and moving to the top. Squeeze and pull the ears very gently, again starting with the lobe and moving to the top and down again. Repeat three times. (The ears are often forgotten in our beauty regime and readily show signs of aging when neglected.)

8 Finally, rub your palms together to create heat and cup them gently over your eyes. Breathe in and out with deep, cleansing breaths from the abdomen and quietly relax.

Try to perform this daily or every other day after your nightly cleansing/toning/moisturizing regime or even for a stress-busting rejuvenation moment at your desk. It works wonders!

Diet

The importance of eating for health and fitness cannot be over-emphasized. If you are diligent and persistent in this, then you can look forward to increased energy levels, better sleep patterns, stronger hair and nails, healthier skin and complexion, whiter and brighter eyes, and increased strength and endurance. Weight loss and having a great body will soon follow as well!

You are what you eat

What you are as a bio-organism is determined exactly by what you eat and drink today, the waste that you eliminate or don't eliminate and how you exercise. This naturally affects how you will look and feel tomorrow. Because of changed eating patterns, researchers now find many of us are not getting even the minimum amounts of the building blocks that our bodies need to be in optimal shape and health.

Everything you do affects the quality of the body you are building for yourself, and living in, day by day. Increasing your exercise levels will go a long way towards turning back your age clock, but in order to exercise efficiently, your body needs the right fuel. It is the combination of these two elements that will produce the best and quickest results.

Eat to stay young

Without a wide variety of healthful foods and attention to eating patterns, no matter how much energy and calories we get from pick-me-up foods, our bodies and minds will deteriorate at a faster rate because we are not able to replicate the dying cells properly, let alone be a strong immune force to keep bugs and illnesses at bay. This is what causes rapid aging, and explains why some go down that route faster than others.

The good news is that, when you take the time to become a student of your own body, and consume a diet rich in nutritious, body-building materials, you can create an environment of great health on all levels, and a totally functional body that is free from disorders. Remember that individual nutrients never work alone – your body is totally dependent on you eating the right mix of chemicals for you to function properly. Even if only a few vitamins or minerals are deficient out of the whole mix, it has a domino effect on your overall well-being.

Lose weight the healthy way

The degree to which you will be able to sculpt your body shape and burn fat is determined by how healthy your engine is. Being over-fat on the outside is a sign that all is not in order on the inside; fat will never need to be stored as excess fuel in an optimally performing body. Carrying excess weight

DITCH ALL THOSE 'AGING' FOODS!

Right at the start, go through all your storecupboards, fridge and freezer and get rid of everything that is 'unauthorized' on this plan:

- 'Beige' foods (pastries, doughnuts, cakes, biscuits, sweet rolls, pies)
- 'White' foods (pasta, white rice, white bread, processed and refined grains)
- Alcohol (put it to the back of the cupboard, reserved for very special occasions)
- Hard cheeses
- Creamy sauces
- Trans fats (found in most margarines, spreads and baked goods)
- Soft drinks (including diet drinks) and fruit drinks
- Cooking oils, margarine, butter, lard, white vegetable fat
- Fried foods, hot dogs, luncheon meats, sausages, spare ribs, salami and so on
- Mayonnaise
- Chips and crisps
- Sweets, cream, ice cream and chocolate
- Sugary breakfast cereals
- Milk and processed dairy products
- Roasts and battered foods
- Convenience meals

is aging to your body – it saps your vitality, puts extra strain on your joints, ligaments and moods, and causes inflammation and damage to your blood vessels.

To gain the anti-aging edge, you need to know that you are more than just a calorie-burning machine. You can lose weight healthily – and more quickly than on a calorie-controlled diet – by sticking to the food principles outlined in this chapter. It is motivational and rewarding to see your fat melt away and the firm, toned lines of your new body take its place. You can transform yourself at any age, and the key to healthy weight loss success is to acknowledge that you are making permanent lifestyle changes, working with your body

and not against it. It is a better way of looking after yourself for life, not just a temporary fix. People successful at keeping their weight off for more than five years have certain characteristics in common. They don't have an unrealistic target weight, they make small changes to their habits rather than major changes and they exercise, plan and face up to problems.

Survive and thrive

Despite all the 'wonder diets' of today, our bodies still thrive best on what our ancestors ate: top-quality animal- and plant-based proteins from wild game and fish, and fresh vegetables, seasonal fruits and seeds – all eaten as close to their natural state as possible. These delicious, unprocessed 'superfoods' limit and repair oxidative damage to our DNA, helping us stay young. We simply do not operate in peak condition on high-density processed grains and sugars.

Your body is consuming calories constantly, and from different sources. It also requires a wide variety of raw materials to renew and maintain its organs, structures and functions. These raw materials you eat are those the body uses to recreate itself. You are in a constant process of degeneration and regeneration, and what you eat and how you exercise today will tip that balance towards better, or worse, health tomorrow. The quality of your nutrition is just as important as the exercise you do.

Perfect balance

Nature has provided us with everything we need not only to survive, but also to thrive! All the vitamins, nutrients, minerals, chemicals and enzymes that go into our bodily make-up have been created in nature in perfect balance and form for us to eat so that we can live at an optimal level of health. An active individual requires a certain balance of macro-nutrients – protein, fats, starchy carbohydrates (grains and root vegetables), fibrous carbohydrates (coloured and leafy vegetables) and simple carbohydrates (fruits).

Most people need to eat about 30 per cent of their food from proteins, 60 per cent from all carbohydrates and 10 per cent from (good) fats (percentages are correct for a balanced intake). Every meal should have carbohydrates, protein and fat in the correct ratios (see pages 74–75 for what should constitute your 'model plate').

Protein

Protein is absolutely essential for the building blocks of the body. Both the *quality* of the protein you eat, determined by the balance of its amino acids, and the *quantity* you eat are important. It keeps your skin clear, your thyroid up to par, your moods stable and your joints working well. Protein also has a positive effect on the satiety centre in the brain and helps regulate appetite. Before you're tempted to eat that cookie, cake or ice cream, have a small piece of grilled chicken breast with lemon or lime juice on it to quell those sweet cravings. It works like magic!

Eat lean proteins at each of your main meals because they have an important effect on metabolism and appetite suppression. Proteins still have a calorific value, so keep to lean fish and poultry breasts in the evening. If you're trying to trim up, egg white is one of the leanest protein sources available, so include one yolk for every three egg whites in your recipes.

There is now a big health question mark over the safety of fish sources around the world. This is due to the toxic pollution and heavy metals present from dumping sewerage into waterways and the run-off from agricultural chemicals. Because of this, whenever you can, choose organic-farmed, wild or line-caught Southern Ocean fish.

Today we consume many times more refined grain foods than our hunter-gatherer ancestors, and much less quality lean protein. It's more than coincidence that obesity was not an issue then!

Healthy sources of protein

Eggs *
Hard-boiled
Omelette (whites only)
Poached
Scrambled (no cheese)

* from chickens or game birds
* eat early in the day

Dairy products
Cottage cheese (low-fat)
Frozen yogurt (with fresh
    fruit)
Protein shake
Yogurt (natural, live,
    organic)

Poultry *
Chicken or turkey breast
Lean minced chicken or
    turkey

* skinless organic

Protein substitutes *
Aduki beans
Almond milk
Beans
Chickpeas
Hummus
Lentils
Quinoa
Quorn™
Soya-based foods
Split peas
Tempeh
Tofu

* vegetarian

Shellfish and other seafood
Crab
Lobster
Mussels
Oysters
Prawns
Scallops
Sea vegetables
Shrimps

Fish
Anchovy
Bluefish
Bream
Carp
Cod
Flounder
Grouper
Haddock
Halibut
Herring
Hoki
Krill
Mackerel
Monkfish
Mullet
Ocean perch
Pollock
Salmon
Sardines
Sea bass
Skate
Sole
Swordfish
Trout
Tuna
Turbot
Whitebait
Whiting

Meat *
Beef
Game
Ham (off the bone)
Lamb
Liver (calf's or lamb's)
Veal

* lean cuts only

Fats

Fats are used by the body to manufacture hormones, carry out brain functions, lubricate the joints and store energy. The amount of essential fat the body needs is very small, but very important. There are too many processed oils and hidden fats in our diet, tipping the natural balance away from the omega-3 healthy fats towards a less healthy predominance of omega-6 fats (found in grains). Choose oils from sustainable sources, such as unprocessed organic linseed, walnut, pumpkin, hemp or soya-bean oil. Avoid hydrogenated margarines, saturated fat, refined processed oils and artificially hardened oils, as these can be high in chemicals that harm our cellular structures. Remember that fats and oils have 9 calories per gram, more than double protein and carbohydrate calorie values, so be very selective with small quantities of good-quality oil when trying to improve your health or to lose weight.

HEALTHY SOURCES OF CARBOHYDRATES (all foods to be organic, where possible)

Fruit (raw; eat early in the day)

Apples	Cranberries	Kiwifruit	Oranges	Quinces
Apricots	Currants	Kumquats	Papaya	Raspberries
Avocados	Dates	Lemons	Passion fruit	Rhubarb
Bananas	Elderberries	Limes	Peaches	Strawberries
Blackberries	Figs	Loganberries	Pears	Tangelos
Blueberries	Gooseberries	Lychees	Pineapple	Tangerines
Boysenberries	Grapefruit	Mangos	Plums	Watermelon
Cherries	Grapes	Melons	Pomegranates	
Crab apples	Guavas	Nectarines	Prunes	

Starchy carbs (eat early in the day)

Barley	Lentils	Parsnips	Rice, wild	Turnips
Beans	Linseeds	Polenta (rough	Rye	Wheat bran flakes
Beetroot	Millet	ground)	Rye crispbreads	Wholemeal pita
Brown rice	Muesli, low in fat,	Poppy seeds	Sesame seeds	Yams
Buckwheat	sugar and salt	Porridge oats	Spelt	
Bulgur wheat	Oat bran	Potatoes	Squashes	
Carrots, cooked	Oatcakes	Pumpkin	Sunflower seeds	
Green peas	Oatmeal	Pumpkin seeds	Sweet potatoes	
Hemp seeds	Okra	Quinoa	Sweetcorn	

Fibrous or non-starchy carbs (eat with all meals)

Alfalfa sprouts	Bok choi	Courgettes	Parsley	Watercress
Artichokes, globe	Broccoli	Cucumber	Peppers, all varieties	
Asparagus	Brussels sprouts	Fennel	Radishes	
Aubergines	Cabbage	Kale	Rocket	
Bamboo shoots	Carrots, raw	Leeks	Shallots	
Bean sprouts	Cauliflower	Lettuce	Spinach	
Beans (runner, green,	Celeriac	Mangetout	Sugar snap peas	
yellow)	Celery, raw	Mushrooms	Swiss chard	
Beetroot tops	Chives	Onions	Tomatoes	

Carbohydrates

Carbs are the main fuel source for the body. Some are simple fast-energy foods, such as those sugars that end with 'ose' on food labels and those found in refined foods. Refined, or processed, carbohydrates, such as white bread, sugary cereals, pasta and noodles made from white flour, are foods where manufacturing has removed the fibre and most of the nutrients – such as the bran and the germ from many grains.

Slow-release complex carbohydrates are crammed full of nutrients and fibre. These are typically vegetables, fruits and wholegrains. Vegetables are not only great de-aging foods but also the supreme diet food. They yield only 25 calories per serving, while fruit has about 60 calories per serving and starches have about 80 calories plus per serving. Compare this to a refined fast-food serving, which can have up to 500 calories! Complex carbohydrates are fantastic for the anti-aging diet, whereas refined carbohydrates leach vitality and health from your system. You can eat unlimited amounts of the non-starchy vegetables listed on page 72.

Dairy products and calcium

More than any other food, milk is controversial; many people believe it's vital in pregnancy, for growing children and for keeping your bones healthy, yet two-thirds of the world's population, including some of the healthiest nations, don't eat dairy products. We have included only a few protein-rich dairy products in these lists because it is thought that many people don't digest them well, leading to allergy symptoms and bloating. If you're worried about calcium intake, concentrate on non-dairy sources such as broccoli, almonds and sardines, or by taking a calcium and vitamin D supplement. There is more calcium in 100 g (4 oz) broccoli than in a glass of milk.

SUPERFOODS TO COMBAT AGING

Longer lives don't mean much if they're not active lives, so here are the top 10 foods to start the changes:

1 Protein – wild fish, lean free-range meats, organic poultry, lentils, tofu, quinoa.

2 Organic vegetables – eaten raw by preference, with as many colours and fibre types as possible: fresh green leafy vegetables such as spinach and silver beet; orange vegetables such as carrots, sweet potatoes and pumpkins, which are rich in carotenes; red foods such as tomatoes, laden with the health-giving lycopene; and green brassicas such as cabbage, broccoli and Brussels sprouts for their anti-cancer effect.

3 Freshly juiced or blended vegetables – blending, rather than just juicing, has the advantage of retaining the fibre content.

4 Fresh organic fruits – eat moderate amounts of all colours.

5 Fresh or dried barley grass and wheat grass

6 Sprouted seeds

7 Organic herbs and spices

8 Organic unprocessed linseed oil

9 Filtered or distilled water

1 0 Herbal teas

The model plate

Protein, carbohydrates, fibre and fats all need to be drip-fed in small, regular and balanced amounts throughout the day to be ingested effectively, and to prevent creating a surplus of any one particular group, which could be turned into fat for storage.

The model plate is an easy way of working out at a glance exactly what should be on your plate for any particular meal, and it can also be used to view your intake over an entire day.

Visualize your plate as being divided into quarters. Each quarter represents a 'serving' in the meal plan opposite. Study this now and look at pages 71 and 72 for charts showing a wide range of healthy sources of protein and carbohydrates.

Plan three days ahead

It's amazing to us that normally switched-on people plan a full appointment diary up to six months in advance, including everything from business meetings to children's educational needs, but there's not one single entry relating to their most fundamentally important asset – their body and health. Everything hinges on being organized for successful body-sculpting fat loss.

Failure to plan leaves you open to poor food choices. On a typical day, rushing home after work, you're often feeling hungry and tired and you just need something to get you by. Quickly purchasing any old thing that looks or smells good to fuel your body is so easy. However, that deli sandwich or French pastry will probably wallop you with as many calories as a full meal, but will leave you feeling hungry again soon afterwards. So planning ahead is very important – there are not a lot of healthy choices when it comes to eating on the run.

If you've been keeping a food diary (see page 44), you'll have got to know your usual habits by writing down your eating patterns. Now is the time to turn things round and plan your meals according to the model plate rules you've just learnt. Every three days, take 10 minutes to write into your diary, planner or notebook every meal you should be eating at the appropriate times for the following three days. To make things even easier for yourself, you can use the same meal that you had for supper one day for your lunch and high tea the next, which can save on both shopping and preparation time. If you're going to be out somewhere, write in either what you'll be taking with you to eat or what you'll be ordering at a restaurant. Use this planner to create your shopping list, to phone restaurants ahead to pre-order your meal and to work out your cooking and food preparation times. You'll be astonished how much easier this will make things! You should be aware that ridding your body of caffeine, sugar and aging foods can leave you with a dull headache or a feeling of fogginess for up to four days as your system detoxifies itself. Drink 2–3 litres (3½–5¼ pints) of water over the course of a day to help aid this cleansing process in the first few days.

Have confidence that you can do it. When you get organized, you will be less fatigued, less rushed, slimmer, toned and in the shape and state of health you always wanted to be.

Your daily meals

You should be aiming to eat little and often. In addition to the four main meals below, include one or two snacks of fruit. You will then be eating five to six times throughout the day.

Fibrous carbs   **Starchy carbs**   **Protein**

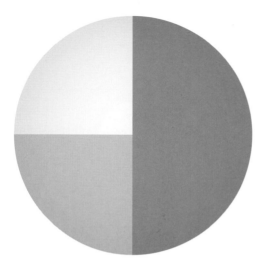

Breakfast Start the day with mostly starchy carbs – about half the meal content (two servings). Include one serving of protein, and another of fibrous carbs. Porridge oats, oat-based muesli and even a cooked breakfast would fit this profile easily.

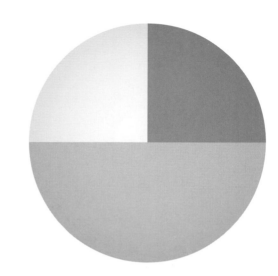

Lunch The next main meal in the day should have more fibrous carbs in it (two servings) and fewer starchy carbs (one serving), as now that your metabolism is fired up, all you need to do is keep it on the boil. Still include a serving of protein.

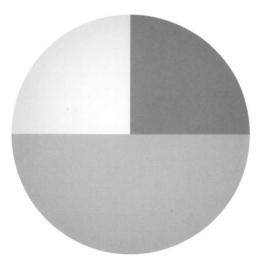

High tea Repeat exactly what you had for lunch in the middle of the afternoon, as your energy requirements will still be the same as you continue with the day's activities.

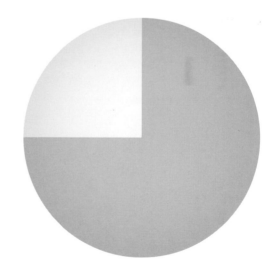

Supper Have your last meal in the early evening. In order to discourage the possibility of taking on calories you're not going to burn, this is the meal in which you cut out starchy carbs altogether. In order to maintain fibre and vitamin intake, however, simply increase the fibrous carbs to three servings. Retain one serving of protein.

Choosing and preparing food

The first job is to have a complete clear-out of all aging foods (see page 69). Then study the healthy sources of protein and carbohydrates listed on pages 71 and 72 and go shopping to stock up on plenty of these ingredients. Plan your meals three days in advance (see page 74). Try to follow the 10-minute rule – no meal should take longer than 10 minutes to prepare – as well as all the advice on food preparation given below. You'll then be well on your way to adopting healthy, nutritious eating habits!

What you need to know

Fish and seafood Generally, seafood is low in fat and high in protein. Much of the damage is done in the preparation, cooking and serving. Avoid frying fish – steam, poach, bake or grill it instead. Avoid adding butter, oil, cream or salt – fresh lemon or a twist or two of black pepper is all that is needed.

Soups Most soups can be created fat-free with a little thought and effort. Many vegetable soups have cream, butter, oil and flour added to create extra texture, taste and thickness to the soup – the best vegetable soup, however, is simply puréed vegetables with only seasoning added. Simmering a little water off the stock or adding potato or rice can thicken it. Unsweetened Greek yogurt should be used as a topping instead of cream or soured cream, and may also be used to give a creamy texture to lobster bisque. Instead of sautéing vegetables in oil for minestrone, they can be sweated in a light stock on a high heat. Thai coconut crab soup should only have a trace of coconut with a chunky fresh stock and vegetable juices. Too often the mixture relies for substance almost totally on coconut milk, which is very high in fat.

Sandwiches Instead of white bread, have a wholemeal, kibbled or Granary roll (single), or, best of all, pita bread. Avoid spreads high in fat, such as butter or margarine. Olive oil spreads, while lower in cholesterol than butter, are still high in fat calories. Cut out cheese, as this is a saturated fat, and mayonnaise, which is made from egg yolks and oil and contains an enormous amount of fat. Stay away from peanut butter,

chocolate and hazelnut spreads – the fat content of these and similar products will go straight on to your hips and stomach! Load your sandwiches with cold meats, salads, tomatoes, grated carrot, chutneys and pickles. Use Greek yogurt as a dressing and flavour with garlic or sweet chilli sauce.

Vegetables You're always a winner when you choose vegetables (greens) to accompany a meal, as they are virtually fat-free. Eat as many fibrous veggies as possible to load up on nutrients, and you can have them grilled, steamed, baked or raw. Use vegetables as the base of any soup stock. For a midday meal, don't be afraid of eating starchy vegetables (potatoes and rice) with your fibrous mixture – you'll need the extra energy to get through the afternoon. For afternoon and evening meals, you could do without the potatoes, bread and rice, selecting instead a healthy and hearty serving of mixed fibrous vegetables.

Salads Basic salad ingredients are healthy, but are usually ruined by dressings containing mayonnaise or oils. There are many fat-free dressings available, or you could try a drizzle of Greek yogurt, balsamic vinegar (no oil) or sweet chilli sauce.

Poultry Chicken, turkey, quail and even ostrich are all of the same biological structure, so these rules apply to all of them. White meat is leanest, and the best choice is breast meat with the skin removed. Dark meat (thighs, wings) has a higher fat content. Avoid crispy-skin chicken, methods such as frying or fricasséeing or any other preparation method that involves oils.

Red meat Always fully trim fat off steak before cooking it. A well-done steak will have more chance of marbled fat being melted down and dripping out of the meat while on the grill. The leanest beef choices are tenderloin, top sirloin, topside and flank. The most fatty cuts are porterhouse, rib, ribeye, T-bone, brisket and chuck steak. Beef mince usually has a very high fat content, so is best avoided unless you pre-boil it to remove excess fat.

Avoid lamb if possible, especially rack, chops and shoulder. Roast lamb is likely to be quite high in fat. Choose leg or loin as the least-fatty cuts.

The least-fatty pork options are loin and tenderloin – sometimes a pork leg steak can be quite lean if the fat is well trimmed before cooking. Avoid chops, rack, rib, shoulder, rump, bacon and processed ham – and *never* eat crackling!

Processed meats Avoid high-fat items such as corned beef, salami, pastrami, mortadella, bresaola or burger patties. Sausages and saveloys tend to be made mainly from fatty offcuts, as does anything containing sausagemeat. Savouries and sausage rolls have fat-rich pastry and contain little in the way of protein or other nutrition.

Desserts Common sense is your main guide here – fruit salads and sorbets are best, though quite sweet, and you'll know to minimize the serving size if you decide to treat yourself to richer fare.

EATING OUT

- Find a restaurant you can return to again and again – the staff will get to know you and your ordering preferences. This makes getting the meal you want easier each time.
- Eat something healthy before you go out. By the time you are seated at the restaurant, you'll be ready to order a smaller-portioned meal without overeating.
- As soon as you're seated, drink a glass of water and take a single roll only to eat while waiting for your order.
- When ordering, ask to have the preparation of unfamiliar dishes explained. Ask which dishes are baked, grilled or fried, and what sauces or dressings they are served with.
- Never hesitate to ask for food to be prepared exactly the way you want it. This may seem awkward at first, but it's an obstacle you'll have to overcome early on for eating healthily to become second nature.

- If you'll be dining at a new restaurant, make the reservation yourself so that you can advise the staff well ahead of your preferences. This also allows you to check if the restaurant can assist with your food choices or not. It may be that you'll have to choose another venue.
- Enquire if the vegetables can be steamed or boiled, and if you would like fewer starchy carbs (potato, pasta, rice), ask if you could have more 'greens' instead.
- Often restaurants serve extra-large helpings. Don't feel bad about asking for a half-portion or starter-sized serving.
- If you're treating yourself to a dessert or sweet, investigate and order the items lowest in fat and sugar.
- Always maintain focus on the benefits of your healthy lifestyle choices: a lean, strong body, a healthy constitution and a bright and vital presence.

Recipe for success

Don't be daunted by all the theory – it's easy to put into practice! You can adapt some of your favourite recipes and start using a few new ones. Variety is key, so don't let yourself get into a pattern of using the same recipes every week.

Adapting existing recipes

Like exercise, eating for a lean and healthy physique has to be incorporated into your routine for life. It does not mean radical changes – your existing recipes or favourite dishes may only need a few changes to make them healthier.

- Add extra fruit, vegetables or wholegrain to increase fibre.
- Increase the variety of vegetables in stews, casseroles and soups to boost the nutritional content.
- Replace bleached grain products, such as white bread, rice and other grains, with organic wholegrains and oats.
- Serve interesting wholegrain side dishes (such as quinoa, bulgur, kasha) instead of noodles or white rice.
- Use coconut oil to wipe your pan or wok before stir-frying. It remains stable when heated, unlike most other oils.
- For browning or sautéeing, use a low-fat cooking spray, wine, stock or lemon juice.
- Use a fat-free stock to replace moisture and flavour lost when you reduce the fat in your recipe. Water, fruit juice and extra herbs or spices work just as well.
- Blot excess fatty residue off meats with kitchen paper.
- Replace mayonnaise with low-fat/sugar natural yogurt.
- Replace minced beef with lean minced chicken or turkey .
- Use a healthier cooking method, such as steaming, baking, grilling or stir-frying.
- Cream cheese can be replaced with low-fat cottage cheese or fromage frais.
- Only use Cheddar cheese for toppings and mix it with rolled oats or wheatgerm.
- Replace garlic salt or onion salt with garlic powder or onion powder, and use unsalted vegetable stocks.
- Fats like oil or butter can usually be cut by one-third.
- Replace some or all of the sugar in recipes with fruit purée or use a low-glycaemic sweetener.
- Replace cream with evaporated skimmed milk.
- Choose canned fruits in water instead of syrup.
- Use fresh-frozen vegetables or fruits (without added sugar), if fresh is unavailable.

Some 10-minute recipe ideas

We've mentioned the 10-minute rule, so here are a few suggestions to get you on your way. Use organic produce where possible. All recipes serve one unless otherwise stated.

Hearty beef bolognese

This will make enough for six medium-sized servings (enough for two days' worth of lunches, high-teas and dinners) and can be frozen for up to a month. Serve with brown rice.

500g organic extra-lean beef mince
2 large onions, sliced
2 peppers, sliced
165 g (5½ oz) mushrooms, sliced
1 x 400 g (13 oz) can chopped tomatoes
1 x 500 g (1 lb) jar of good quality organic ready-made Bolognese sauce
1 x 400 g (13 oz) can of kidney beans
500g (1 lb) packet of organic frozen mixed vegetables.
ready-made chilli sauce or tabasco to taste
1 tablespoon low-fat natural yogurt or low-fat sour cream, to serve

Boil the mince in a pan of water, reduce the heat and simmer for 5 minutes, then drain.

Fry the onions, peppers and sliced mushrooms in a dry pan. Add the mince, chopped tomatoes, Bolognese sauce, kidney beans and frozen vegetables. Add chilli sauce or Tabasco to taste. Simmer until ready to serve.

Spoon on the yogurt or sour cream before serving.

Lumberjack rolls™

These mighty rolls are great to pack for travelling or lunch at the office and make an easy meal at home. Filling quantities will vary depending on the size of bread used.

1 medium organic baguette or small organic baton loaf
sandwich pickle, chutney or mustard of choice
organic hummus
pre-cooked organic chicken breast
cooked beetroot, sliced
boiled eggs, sliced
tomatoes, sliced
lettuce or salad leaves of choice
carrot, grated
courgette, grated
pepper, thinly sliced
thin slice camembert
raw onion, sliced into rings
black pepper or Thai sweet chilli dipping sauce, to flavour

Split the loaf in half horizontally, leaving the back edge intact to act as a hinge. Remove the soft bread from both halves and discard, leaving a hollow crust.

Spread chutney, pickle or mustard on the inside of one half of the crust and organic hummus on the inside of the other half.

Fill the insides with the remainder of the ingredients, flavouring with black pepper or a little Thai sweet chilli dipping sauce. Close the two halves before eating.

The ultimate "turn back your age clock" health shake

This is a fantastic way to eat raw vegetables and fruit, which contain powerful anti-oxidants often knocked out during cooking. Use your imagination with the ingredients but keep the balance higher in vegetables than fruit where possible.

½ pint (8 fl oz) chilled water
500 g (1 lb) of fresh uncooked organic vegetables, such as
     broccoli, carrot, cabbage, cauliflower, beetroot, celery
2.5 cm (1 inch) cube ginger
75 g (3 oz) frozen raspberries, strawberries or blueberries
     (or a mixture of all three)
1½ tablespoons of whey protein powder (any flavour)
125 ml (4 fl oz) organic natural yogurt

Blend the ingredients in a heavy duty blender until the mixture is the consistency of a smooth thickshake. Serve.

For extra vitality and zest you can add a splash of organic Aloe Vera juice, a teaspoon of apple cider vinegar, 1 tsp dried wheat or Barley grass and 1 tsp spirulina.

Taking supplements

The principal aim of turning back your age clock is to create glowing, abundant health and boundless energy. There's a huge difference between feeling 'just OK' and feeling 'fantastic', and although eating well will take you a long way towards achieving optimal health, in order to climb up to the top rung of the anti-aging ladder the consensus among the world's leading researchers is that you also need to take some supplements.

Why do I need supplements?

Diet alone cannot satisfy the body's nutrient needs from an anti-aging or athletic perspective. Daily supplementation provides powerful protection against age-accelerating nutritional deficiencies by supplying all the important 'building blocks' needed by the body for optimum function. The human body requires a staggering 100,000 different proteins, essential minerals, trace elements, vitamins and enzymes, plus thousands of nutrients that haven't even been discovered yet, in order to operate at peak efficiency. It is well documented that not even one in ten of us suceeds in meeting this ideal level of nutrition.

All of our energy problems, weight problems, diseases and illnesses have their roots in malnourishment at some level, and this, unfortunately, gets progressively worse with age. What you eat and when you eat affects all your cells and their operating ability, and therefore every aspect of your being, from mood, energy levels and food cravings right through to thinking and learning capacity, fertility, sex drive, sleeping habits, immunity and general health.

Improving your diet is one step towards better health and fitness – now you need to boost your chances even further by making sure you're getting all the vitamins and minerals your body needs every day.

Combining supplements and diet

It is important to recognize the need to use vitamin and mineral supplements as just that – 'supplements' to an existing optimal diet. They are designed to take care of the shortfall and the depletion in nutrient profiles brought on through modern growing techniques, storage and methods of manufacturing of some of these foods, as well as to support our immune systems as they battle against the noxious and

WHAT TO TAKE

Most people know we need vitamins and minerals, but not that we need so many a day. They take a supplement for a few weeks and then forget because they don't notice any significant improvements – there are normally only around 20 different components in the average vitamin/mineral tablet. But we need 76 vitamins and minerals to ensure good health, plus amino acids and oils. So, as a minimum, you need to take the following every day:

- a multivitamin supplement
- a multimineral and trace element supplement
- a vitamin C supplement
- an omega-3 capsule
- a calcium-magnesium supplement (if required)

Because this is a very specialist subject, however, always consult with a specialized professional in nutritional anti-aging medicine prior to embarking on any supplementation programme.

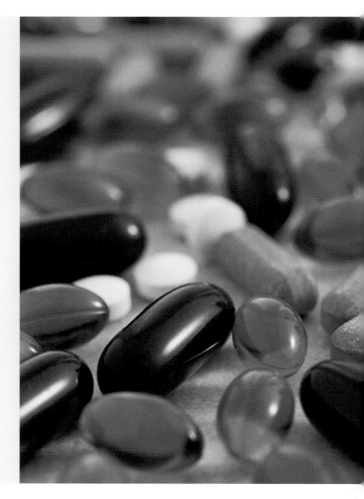

toxic environments most of us unavoidably find ourselves living in today.

Strangely enough, we have a situation where many adults and children are malnourished in a sea of plenty. We are drowning in an ocean of calories, but with too few nutrients. In study after study, it has been found that less than 10 per cent of people get enough nutrients for optimal health from their daily diet. For example, a daily intake of 5,000 calories of fat is necessary to get the amount of vitamin E needed for an anti-aging effect; and, to get the optimum intake of chromium, you would have to take in more than 12,000 calories a day! A daily intake of 2,400 calories is needed just to reach the RDA for zinc and magnesium (the government's guideline 'recommended daily allowance' or RDA is intended to stop you getting disease rather than to indicate the amount for optimal health and radiance).

A long life is of no use if it's lived in poor health. Deliberately going for long periods without eating and then

bingeing is a recipe for malnourishment and weight gain. Another mistake is taking just one specific vitamin, as this can lead to imbalances. For good health, the balance of essential vitamins and minerals should be taken together. Like an orchestra, they work together within the body and interact to aid maintenance, regeneration and repair.

The anti-aging workout

When we become more active and improve our fitness, it's much easier to create a balance within our lives and to let go of the old habits that may have been accelerating aging. The moment you start to eat well and exercise to the right anti-aging formula, you begin to feel great. As you begin to change from the inside out, you'll not only feel better but you'll also begin to see results in the mirror in as little as four weeks!

Before you start

First, go back and read pages 20–23 to remind you of all the benefits of exercise. The rejuvenator circuits in this chapter have been constructed for maximum benefit in minimal time.

Even when you think you're very busy, it yields such substantial benefits to how you look and feel that you'll more than make up for the time you take in doing it. The meal structure set out in the diet chapter also saves lots of time by cooking meals only once a day, in the evening, and prevents wasted time buying lunches during the day that may be less than ideal anyway. Imagine feeling twice as energetic, slimmer and more physically vibrant than ever before. Do you need any more reasons to make the time to boost your body? It's false economy to be too busy to exercise regularly and eat well, because making the time gives you time!

Another trick to keeping your exercise plan on track is to work out in the morning. Often people plan to exercise in the afternoon or evening, only to cancel because something has come up, and the opportunity is lost again for another day. Interruptions are unlikely to happen early in the morning; it helps you to stay consistent and gives that sluggish metabolism a massive fat-burning hit from the start. Because exercise stimulates the 'feel-good' hormones – endorphins – you'll be set up for the day, feeling both calm and stress-free. Go to bed 15 minutes earlier at night, and set your alarm to go off 15 minutes earlier in the morning, and soon it will become part of your morning hygiene ritual.

DEEP-BREATHING TECHNIQUE

A person at rest breathes 12–15 times a minute, but a lot of us miss out on vital energy and the detoxifying benefit of oxygen through poor posture and the habit of breathing small, shallow breaths. You can strengthen your lungs with aerobic exercise (see pages 86–87) and correct breathing techniques. The lower third of the lungs is the most richly concentrated with oxygen-exchange units, followed by the middle section, so you must breathe deeply whenever possible. Expand your abdomen during inhalation, allowing maximum air to be brought into this lower area, and contract it as you exhale. Remember this technique as you perform any kind of exercise.

Safety first

As with any other significant change in lifestyle, it's essential to approach the exercise circuits in this chapter with caution and common sense. If you're suffering from any underlying health problems, or you take things much too fast, you could do yourself physical – possibly irreparable – damage. Make sure you get the all-clear from your doctor before you begin the exercise programme, and always follow the instructions given – they are designed to build up your exercise levels gradually, safely and effectively to create a slim, fit, toned, healthy new you! Warming up, stretching and cooling down are all essential elements of any exercise session.

Different types of exercise

The rejuvenator circuits are designed to build up your muscle strength, which is one of the best anti-aging tools, but you will also need to exercise your cardiovascular system through aerobic exercise (see pages 86–87), your memory and your vision (see pages 88–89) for optimum results in turning back your age clock.

Remember your training diary

Don't forget to plan your exercise sessions in your diary (see page 44) as you go along, and stick to them. If for any reason you miss a session, you must record this in your diary too. This will alert you to any regular stumbling blocks, and you can then work out a way around them in order to keep up with the programme.

Aerobic exercise

Any type of exercise that is moderately vigorous in intensity and can be sustained for a reasonable length of time is aerobic, which literally means 'with oxygen'. It increases the body's need for oxygen and thereby improves the capability of the cardiovascular system – the heart, lungs and blood vessels – to supply oxygen to the muscles. Before embarking on any new type of exercise programme, remember that you should always check with your doctor.

Have a look at the options described here, and pick the ones that appeal to you most. You'll need to enjoy what you're doing, as when you're on the master plan you'll be performing these activities regularly for sustained periods. Try to vary your aerobic activity so that you don't become bored or stale. The most important aspect of all exercise is to incorporate things that you like to do, and want to do, as this will keep you motivated.

How intense is your exercise?

Intensity reflects how hard you are working in any one exercise. When you do an activity harder or faster, you add to its intensity. As a guide, your aerobic training zone should be 60–80 per cent of your theoretical maximum heart rate (MHR). To calculate your MHR, simply subtract your age from the number 220. For example, if your age is 40, the calculation should look like this:

$220 - 40 = 180 \times 0.6 = 108$ (60 per cent of MHR)

$220 - 40 = 180 \times 0.8 = 144$ (80 per cent of MHR)

So your ideal training heart rate should be between 108 and 144 beats per minute.

Brisk or 'power' walking

If power walking is your choice, walk briskly enough to raise your heart rate into your aerobic training heart rate zone. The Talk Test is a simple tool for assessing your intensity. After you have warmed up and got into your stride, you should be breathing harder and starting to perspire. At this time you should not be able to hold a chatty conversation, but only utter a few brief sentences. At the same time you should not be so breathless that you cannot say anything. If you cannot easily achieve this intensity by walking, then try hill walking or moving up to a slow jog.

Jogging or running

Jogging or sprint running is one of the best calorie-burning aerobic activities. We find those new to running try to go too fast for too long and quickly burn out. Start very slowly and get used to the feel of jogging. It is natural for your body to feel heavy and cumbersome at first, but this soon disappears and you begin to feel fluid and streamlined. To progress, set yourself a distance and a time and work at beating your best in one of these areas each workout. A pedometer is a great motivational tool when beginning walking or jogging.

Cycling

Cycling is a non-weight-bearing exercise that is especially good for the over-weight or elderly person. Cycling is a great way to get around as well as burn calories, although you do need to increase your intensity and distance when cycling. If cycling outside is not your thing, home exercise cycles can be a good choice and will give variety to your routine, particularly during the wet winter months. It is important to adjust the height of the seat so that the leg at the bottom of the down-stroke is almost but not quite completely extended when the foot is on the pedal. Spin classes are another great way to get an intense workout while cycling. You can still work at your own level, but be motivated by an instructor.

Rowing

This is a great workout, as it uses leg and upper body strength as well as improving cardiovascular fitness. Always start your rowing session slowly to warm up for 5–10 minutes. Make sure your posture is correct, and only after you are fully warmed up start your intense exercise session. If using an indoor rowing machine, go for one with a calorie, speed, distance and time display. It keeps you honest!

Elliptical trainers and treadmills

These are useful, as they accommodate all levels of fitness and you can accurately gauge your improvements. Treadmills are quite different from running outside where your calorie burn-off will be different, as you have the resistance of the weather and terrain to make you work harder. The treadmill also has a motor driving the belt for you!

Do not hold on to the handrails when working out. They are there to stop you falling off the machine, not to hold you up.

Swimming

Swimming is also a non-weight-bearing cardiovascular exercise. It is not as easily accessible as jogging or walking but because of its low impact and non-weight-bearing qualities, it is suitable for all ages and those with recovering injuries. Take care not to pig out after a swim, as this particular exercise can stimulate appetite.

Dancing or aerobics classes

As well as cardiovascular benefits, these classes have the added bonus of working your brain activity and coordination, which are so important to challenge if you want to turn back the age clock. Watch the class first and don't be afraid to ask questions before you choose one. Be consistent, because as you get to know the moves, you really can start to enjoy the whole experience. After mastering the basics, you can learn other dances or advance to more challenging exercise classes.

Skipping

This is the most inexpensive and portable of all the cardiovascular equipment. Skipping is not a very high-profile exercise, but it is a wonderfully intense workout and a high calorie burner for those who have built up a good fitness level.

CAUTION

You should wait at least 60 minutes after a full meal before engaging in any kind of intensive cardiovascular exercise while digestion takes place. The larger the amount of food you eat, the longer the time you should wait before beginning aerobic exercise.

Other aerobic exercise options

There are an enormous amount of additional cardiovascular exercises, such as hiking, hill climbing, cross-country skiing, rollerblading, basketball and tennis. Regardless of what activity you choose, they all have their own cardiovascular benefits. Whatever exercise type you may be considering, the following should be your guide to choosing:

1 Does the exercise offer a sustained and repetitive movement using large muscle groups, such as your legs?
2 Are you able to maintain an intensity of 60–80 per cent of your maximum heart rate?
3 Does your activity allow you to be active continually for at least 30–45 minutes?
4 Can you continue with this activity 4–5 days a week in order to keep improving?

Vision and memory exercises

Our head is the control panel for our body, yet we tend to forget about the health of our brain when it comes to the quest for looking better. Keeping your brain, memory and vision thriving begins with an anti-aging diet, the correct exercise and supplementation. Being aware and detecting subtle shifts in your balance of health early on is the key to prevention.

Vision

While these exercises may not necessarily improve your vision, they can help maintain your best eyesight level during the day and keep those muscles strong and agile.

It's more important to do the exercises regularly than to do them for a long time. Even 30–60 seconds of eye movement every hour is very helpful. For example, when your computer takes its own time to do something, most people just swear at the thing and waste the time, but you can use that time to make a few circles with your eyes. Even on the first day you do this, you should notice that when you finish working your eyes aren't as tired as usual.

Consult your optician if you believe there may be a problem before doing any of these exercises. When doing them, make sure you're not facing anybody, or at least make sure they know you're doing eye exercises. If you wear glasses or contact lenses, you'll need to remove them before you start.

- Sit about 15 cm (6 in) from a window. Make a mark on the glass at your eye level (a small sticker would be perfect). Look through this mark and focus on something in the far distance for 10–15 seconds; then focus on the mark again.
- Roll your eyes clockwise, then anticlockwise. Do this five times, and blink in between each time.
- Hold a pencil in front of you at arm's length. Move your arm slowly to your nose, and follow the pencil with your eyes until you can keep it in focus. Do this 10 times.
- Imagine you are standing in front of a really big clock. Look at the middle of the clock. Then look at any hour mark, without turning your head. Look back at the centre. Then look at another hour mark. Do this at least 12 times so that you cover every hour mark.

Memory

Our capacity for memory in the short term is generally thought to be between five and nine pieces of information for at least 30 seconds. This is why it is easy to forget somebody's name without actively reinforcing it into your long-term memory.

Just as we take exercise for our body, it is of great benefit to test your memory and thinking skills continually. Good mental workouts include crossword puzzles, sudoku, brainteasers and trivia games, or even the challenge of learning a new language. These will all help to flex your mental muscles. You can also practise the recording and retrieval of information with the exercises below.

- Ask a friend to read strings of randomly selected numbers and letters to you and then repeat them in the exact order. Start with 5 items, then 10, then 15 and so on.
- Try doing your normal everyday tasks in a different way. It could be something as simple as using the computer mouse or texting with your 'off' hand, for example.
- Ask a friend to think of six unrelated objects and name them out loud while you try to remember them. Now get them to say a six-letter word to you. Spell that word to them backwards. Now try to recall all the objects on the list.
- In turn, read each of the following groups of letters and then quickly cover or turn over the page and write down as many as you can remember:

r d h u t i l m f e z s p o

g n i c n i s l t a q i n

- Look at an action picture from a magazine or book. Study it for 10 seconds, carefully taking in all the minute details, trying to remember as much of the picture as you can.

After the 10 seconds, turn over the page and write down as many details about the picture as you can remember. Look at the picture again and compare your recollections of it.

- This exercise will help to improve your visual as well as your verbal memory while reading the newspaper. Pick a story and read it through only once. Then write down the answers to the following questions: who is featured, what

did they say, when did the event take place, where did the event occur? Try to recall as much of it as you possibly can. You will then find that you read articles with a great deal more concentration and awareness, and this will carry over into conversations, learning names and so on.

The rejuvenator circuits

No matter how old you are, you can expect rapid changes to occur within the first two weeks of starting your rejuvenator circuit exercise programme according to the eight-week master plan (see pages 42–53).

During that time there's a lot going on: your brain is making new connections to muscle and the wiring of your nervous system is being reorganized so that it can coordinate and recruit your muscles to exercise more efficiently. It is also stimulating parts of your muscle that through time may have fallen idle.

By the six-week mark, you'll feel dynamic from top to toe. You'll have lost fat from all over your body and your muscles will be toned and more defined. After eight weeks, your skin will be smooth and glowing, the cellulite and flab will have all but disappeared and you will enjoy new slender tone in places you never thought possible. De-aging is restoring the body back to optimal health inside and out; it is the magic of awaking every day with a total sense of purpose, energy and well-being. Always seek to improve your performance every day – don't forget that when it comes to improving your health, if you do the same, you'll stay the same!

How the circuits work

Over the many years that we have worked with clients, we have identified the most critical areas that need the most urgent attention. These very effective exercises are designed to hit on those aging hot spots of the body. You cannot 'spot-lose' body fat, but you can spot-tone, tighten and realign to a more youthful figure. The circuits are very time-efficient – just 20 minutes in the morning, and that's it for the day! We have created an exercise for every part of your body, no matter what your fitness level.

Experts now agree that to burn calories and stay fit and strong you must create lean muscle for long-term control of your health and your shape. These circuits speed up the metabolism of even the most hardened dieter and provide a very convenient routine that even busy people can fit into their schedule. Muscle knows no age, and it is muscle that determines your metabolism!

Our circuits utilize the peripheral heart action principle. The sequence works by not only alternating between the upper and lower body muscles, increasing the blood flow to the working limbs in these areas, but also between the front and back muscle groups for maximum fat burn and tone. This is not an overload programme to bulk muscle, but it is a total body workout and we guarantee it will leave you firmer and leaner than ever before. It is very targeted and ideal for short, intense workouts that give rapid results. It is also very easy to move straight from one exercise to another.

Peripheral arterial disease is a very common condition affecting many people in middle to later life, so besides burning body fat and toning those disused or aging muscles, this form of exercise will also keep your arteries elastic and young.

The rejuvenator circuits are ideal for helping to improve the balance of hormones in both men and women, in particular with respect to levels of your own natural anti-aging growth hormone which, diminishes quickly with a sedentary lifestyle.

CALORIE-BURNING OPPORTUNITIES™

In everyday activities, always think in terms of seeking extra calorie-burning opportunities (CBOs™). This means walking rather than driving that short distance to the shops, running up stairs or taking them two at a time, using a hand whisk rather than an electric one and so on. Extra calorie-burning opportunities™ can amount to an extra 350 calories a day, approximately 15 kg or (33 lb) of fat loss a year.

- Become a fidget – you will burn many more calories.
- Jog the dog for 10 minutes each day.
- Try not to sit still for more than half an hour during the day.
- Get off the bus or train one or two stops before your regular stop.
- If using public transport, always stand instead of sitting when travelling to work.
- Use the bathroom on another floor at work.
- Walk or be active for at least 20 minutes in your lunch hour.
- Walk to the corner shop for the weekend paper.
- Mow your lawn.
- Play with the children instead of just watching them.
- Walk or cycle with the children to school.
- Cycle or rollerblade instead of driving.
- Throw away the remote controls and get out of your chair to change channels.
- While watching television, perform some target-toning exercises in the advert breaks.
- Park as far from the shopping centre as you can.
- Walk an extra lap of the shopping centre before you load up with parcels.
- Carry groceries to the car instead of using the trolley.
- Go dancing instead of going out for a meal.
- Take the stairs instead of the lift.
- Sign up for a charity walk or run.

How to use the circuits

Follow the master plan (see pages 42–53) for guidance on when to perform each circuit throughout the eight weeks.

With each circuit, start with any one exercise and perform repetitions of the movement as many times as you are comfortable with in the set time (30 seconds each exercise to begin with). When the time is up for that exercise, simply change to the next one and, once again, perform the movement for the time allowed. Move your way through the exercises in a similar fashion to 'musical chairs' until you have completed them all, at which point you should start all over again. Continue until the total time for the workout session is completed (see The Master Plan on pages 42–53).

The beauty of this workout is that there is no setting up of equipment separately for each exercise, or waiting on a specific resting time before you proceed to the next exercise. The entire circuit can be completed over 10, 20, 30 or 40 minutes, and you have targeted all the problem areas of an aging physique with just the one workout.

Get inspired and keep challenging yourself as soon as it feels slightly easy – squeeze out more repetitions or add some extra weight. If you have time, you can do an extra lap of your circuit. Because of the way it is specially formulated, it will not dangerously overwork any one body area.

Aerobic activities

A healthy body is one that is balanced, toned, strong and flexible. Every other day when you are not doing a circuit or the target-training programme, make time in your day for aerobic activities (see pages 86–87), starting with at least 15 minutes' exercise, and gradually building up to 50 minutes. Choose an activity that fits into your lifestyle, and one you can maintain.

✔

✗

HINTS AND TIPS

- You should feel you have worked your muscles to the limit after each set. The exercises should feel challenging, or your body will have no reason to change.
- Do not use momentum to swing the weights. Control the movement all the way up and resist on the way down.
- Completely flex and extend the area you are working on, but don't snap-lock the joint when using weights.
- Be consistent with your programme.
- Keep your speed up with no resting between stations.
- Keep an exercise diary filled in every day.
- Maximize calorie-burning, on top of muscle toning, with the bonus of 'afterburn'. This means you not only burn calories during your workout but also afterwards.
- The more muscle groups you work, the better. The circuits are designed for maximum effect in minimum time for every part of your body.

Warming up

This is essential to prepare your body for more strenuous work. You may choose your warm-up – try five minutes of light skipping or hula-hooping, which is now becoming fashionable within the fitness industry. Alternatively, you could prepare your body by doing a light pace around the first circuit to warm your muscles, ligaments and tendons through the specific movements you are about to launch into.

Cooling down and stretching

Cool down gently to get your heart rate back to normal and stretch the muscles. An easy way to do this is to do another slower and lighter lap of the circuit to finish off with. Stretches are an important part of your programme, as being flexible equals effortless and fluid postural movement, so don't neglect to go through the simple routine we've put together for you on pages 132–139. This can be done every time you finish any type of exercise.

There are over 450 muscles in the body and muscle makes up at least 40 per cent of our body weight. It is important to strengthen and stretch all of these through their full range of movement, otherwise tightening and weakness can occur giving rise to the stiffness we often wrongly diagnose as advancing age. It's not just about feeling fitter and stronger, it's about reducing body fat, looking leaner and taller, and improving confidence and posture.

Making it easier or harder

If you are new to exercise and want to make it easier, perform only one circuit or each toning exercise for 20 seconds rather than 30. You can avoid muscle soreness by beginning this way and progressing gradually. Performing the rejuvenator circuit with aerobic exercise on alternate days gives the skeletal muscles time to repair so that they become progressively stronger and toned. They should feel a little sore after your circuit, but not painful. Follow the photographs for good form; it is important to avoid injury. Poor exercise technique can also prevent you from seeing the results you seek.

If you are already seeing great results and you have reached a level where you want to make your workout harder, increase the circuit time and the intensity. You can also increase your weights or work at each station for 60–90 seconds.

Equipment

The circuits are designed to be done just about anywhere, but there are a few items of equipment that will help you immensely in your quest to turn back your age clock. For example, you can put together an excellent home gym with a set of good-quality, adjustable dumbbells and a stability ball. Compared to most home exercise equipment, the versatility of these two items makes them a bargain.

Pedometer

A pedometer is a small device for counting your steps that can be attached to your belt or clothing. It's an excellent fitness tool, being your daily reminder of how active you actually are. You should be aiming for at least 10,000 steps a day to prevent weight gain and to maximize health, and over 15,000 steps if you are in a serious fat-burning phase of your training. It is also a vital tool for understanding how important incidental exercise is in getting back into great shape.

Imagine the difference in calorie expenditure if you walk to the shops, expending 315 calories, rather than deciding to order goods on the internet and burning only 18 calories. If you consume 28 g (1 oz) of mixed nuts (174 calories) for morning break, your pedometer will tell you that you'll need to run continuously for 19 minutes to burn those calories off again. Only a few calories extra each minute can add up to millions in a year!

Dumbbells

Dumbbells are great for turning back your age clock because they work within the range and flexibility of movement you currently have. You don't have to fit into a one-size-fits-all

> Only a few calories extra each minute can add up to millions in a year!

machine, and they give you a more versatile workout. They allow your joints to work independently on each side of the body – it's amazing how unbalanced our strength levels are between the left and right side of the body. They naturally increase your range of movement and help enhance coordination, control and balance. You can perform an infinite variety of exercises with a set of adjustable dumbbells, increasing the weight as and when you feel able to progress, and by a wide variety of increments – all from the one piece of equipment!

Stability (Swiss) ball

You can adapt most gym exercises to be done on a stability ball instead of a bench for convenience, but also for greater variation. Because of the naturally unstable surface of the ball, your body is forced to recruit more muscle fibres when performing even simple exercises. Gaining strength, tone, flexibility, coordination and balance are basic requirements for creating the body of your future, and the stability ball is a great all-round tool for getting you right on track in a convenient and cost-effective way.

Look for a ball to suit your height (to double check you have the correct size of ball, when sitting on the ball make sure your knees are at right angles):

Height	Correct ball size
Below 1.6 m (5 ft 3 in)	53 cm (21 in)
1.6–1.8 m (5 ft 3 in–6 ft)	65 cm (26 in)
Over 1.8 m (6 ft)	75 cm (30 in)

Shoes

You are committing to rejuvenating your body, so even when you are training indoors, make sure you have a good pair of training shoes to support your own foot structure correctly. When you slip them on, you'll start to feel that you're getting into the right mindset, knowing you are about to change your physique for the better. Well-fitting training shoes will also benefit you if you decide to take a training day outdoors. Shop around for an ideal fit for your foot type. A low, medium or a high arch will affect how you land on your feet when walking.

Support bra

If you're a woman, a well-fitting bra is essential when doing any exercise or fitness activity. Many of the exercises we've suggested do target the chest because the breasts need all the support they can get, from the muscle structures underneath as well as external structural clothing. Too frequently, we see women running and exercising without adequate support, and as their bodies travel in one direction, their breasts head off in another! Over time, with this lack of attention the natural support structures under and around the breasts weaken and stretch. Droopy breasts are aging, and a good-quality, supportive sports bra will help any strain on the tissues.

Music

Any prop that helps you stay on track while you get good habits formed is of great value to the consistency of your exercise programme. Play some favourite music that you like, preferably with a hard, driving beat. This helps keep your pace up, and really energizes and motivates you. The more energy and intensity you can incorporate into your rejuvenator circuits, the better the results will be.

Cardio pump

Butt blaster

Press-up

Reverse sit-up

Floor cycling

Sofa squat

Batwing blitz

Butt lifter

Bodyweight circuit

On the master plan, you'll begin with this bodyweight circuit, designed to slim you down and trim you up. At the start, you'll work for 20–30 seconds on each activity and perform this circuit every second day for two weeks. To challenge you further, you'll then change to completing 20 repetitions of each activity instead of 30 seconds for another two weeks. Make sure you don't stop until you have completed 20 repetitions, regardless of how long it takes. Try to be as quick as possible – after all, we do want you to break into a sweat!

Cardio pump

An extremely functional activity, stair climbing involves elements of strength, balance, coordination, posture and fitness – a good all-round fitness conditioner! If you only have a short set of steps, step briskly up and down off the second step for 30 seconds, or use a secure box or step about 36 cm (14 in) high.

1 Begin climbing up the stairs two at a time until you reach the landing.

2 If there are further stairs on from here, continue climbing until you reach the top of the flight. If not, simply return to the bottom (one stair at a time) and then repeat for the allotted time.

3 As your fitness improves, increase your pace.

TIPS

Pay attention to your posture. Avoid looking down or slumping as you fatigue. Keep your back upright and tummy muscles tight. Don't hang on to the banister or assist your legs by pushing down on the thighs with your hands. Each time you come to this station, lead with a different leg, as you will notice a difference in strength between them.

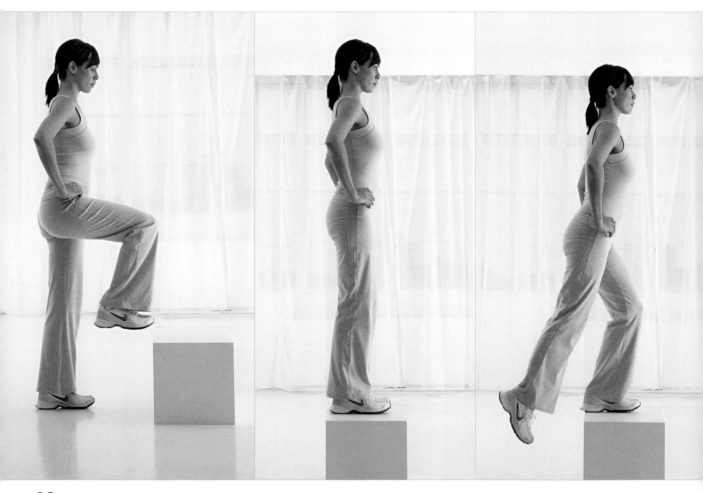

Butt blaster

This move is a proven winner! You'll find it will tie in the lower back, buttocks and hamstrings all at once, giving a beautiful shape to the back of the thighs, and emphasizing clear and firm definition of the lower cheek line.

1 Lie on a soft mat, place your feet on a bench or chair and bend your knees. Arms should be by your sides with the palms facing down.

2 Breathing in, tighten your abdominals and buttocks, then exhale and lift your hips up off the floor. Keep raising your buttocks up until your body is in a straight line, then squeeze your buttocks and lower yourself back to the starting position.

3 Repeat as many times as you can for 20–30 seconds. You should now really feel the blood pulsing into those lazy hamstring muscles. This is a great way to bring vital nutrients to the stagnant area of cellulite.

TIPS

Pause and hold that hard squeeze in the buttocks at the top of the movement. Keep this movement controlled. Once you have got the feel for this exercise, you could try it with your feet placed on a stability ball for an extra core challenge.

Sofa squat

This is a serious compound move for adding great tone to the legs, especially a shapely sweep to the thighs, as well as the buttocks. You'll find an improvement in hip stability, inner thigh tone and lower back strength as additional benefits from this universal conditioner.

1 Stand about 30 cm (1 ft) out from a sofa or armchair, facing into the room. Your feet should be no wider than shoulder-width apart.

2 With the arms either across the chest or extended out to the front for balance, take a deep breath in and squat down until your bottom lightly touches the sofa cushion, keeping the knees in line with your feet.

3 Without resting, or sinking all the way down, immediately reverse the movement, exhaling forcefully as you rise. Don't allow the legs to fully straighten or snap-lock the knees at the top.

4 Repeat without pausing until you reach your target.

TIPS

Always keep your back straight and head well up so that the body is as upright as possible and your airway open and clear. When squatting, it's important for correct knee alignment to ensure your knees bend out directly over your second toes. Always try to keep your feet flat on the floor without raising up on the toes – think of pushing the ground away with your heels as you are rising up. As soon as your bottom touches the cushion, immediately rise up again. The purpose of the exercise will be lost if you continue all the way down, lean back, put your feet up and read a magazine or watch the television in the middle!

Batwing blitz

Our triceps are often referred to as 'bat wings' and are notoriously weak. We rarely straighten our arms against resistance in our automated society, so they begin to show aging rather quickly. The dip is an excellent exercise for toning and tightening the backs of the arms.

1 Place your hands shoulder-width apart, fingers forward, on the edge of a chair or bench.

2 Extend your legs, but ensure you maintain a very slight bend at the knee, avoiding lock-out. Placing one heel on top of the toes of the other foot will keep the movement strict.

3 Inhale and lower your body with your elbows directed backwards until they form an angle of 90 degrees.

4 Exhale forcefully as you drive upwards, straightening the arms fully.

5 Change foot position halfway through the set of repetitions so that the other one is on top.

TIPS

Ensure you have a stable platform to work from – sometimes it helps to have the back of the chair against the wall. Take care not to 'snap' the elbows into a locked position. You should reach full extension in a smooth controlled manner. Keep your body close to the chair to prevent 'swinging' out. For an advanced variation, put your feet on a stability ball.

Butt lifter

This is possibly the best exercise for targeting the glutes, thighs, hip strength and core muscles, and for improving your balance all in one movement. Do you ever wonder why your bottom doesn't look as pert as it did when you were younger? Well, it doesn't get worked out as much as it used to, and it is an area that needs specific exercises to get it tight and toned again. Never accept anything less than how you want to be – you can lift it back to its natural youthful shape! The walking lunge is superior to a static lunge, and is the version our celebrity clients come back to time and again for tightening up legs and glutes in preparation for those sneaky paparazzi beach pics! Once you are confident and smooth with this exercise, simply carry a light dumbbell in each hand to increase the resistance (see page 112).

> *Once you are confident and smooth with this exercise, simply carry a light dumbbell in each hand to increase the resistance.*

1 Standing with your hands on your hips, take a bold and long step forwards, placing the front foot flat on the floor. The rear heel should come up and remain on the toes.

2 Sink down and forwards until the back knee is about 5 cm (2 in) off the ground. You should feel a good stretch through the top of the trailing thigh, and the front foot should be positioned well out in front so that the knee is not protruding beyond the toes. Your body should be dead upright.

3 In a fluid, smooth movement, drive up and off the back foot, swinging straight through into the next step.

4 Continue forwards until you have completed your required target on each leg.

TIPS

As you sink into each movement, try to lean back with your upper body as far as you can to increase flexibility in the hip and thigh. It's not a thigh-bulking exercise as long as you remember to stretch right out and sink low.

Floor cycling

A very effective exercise for working the upper 'six-pack' muscles, flattening the stomach and developing strength through the lower abdominal muscle wall all in one movement. The bicycle exercise is the best move to target the rectus abdominis and the obliques (the waist), according to a study done by the American Council on Exercise.

1 Lie face up on the floor and lace your fingers behind your head.

2 Bring your knees in towards your chest and lift your shoulder blades off the ground without pulling on your neck.

3 Straighten your left leg out to about a 30-degree angle, while crunching up and turning your upper body to the right, bringing your left elbow towards your right knee.

4 Switch sides, bringing your right elbow towards your left knee.

5 Continue alternating sides in a 'pedaling' motion for 20–30 seconds or 20 repetitions, according to the master plan.

TIPS

Don't pull the neck forwards with your hands.

> ' A very effective exercise for working the upper 'six-pack' muscles '

Reverse sit-up

The reverse sit-up is a wonderful exercise for beginners if you have little strength in your abdominals and you find raising your torso off the floor in a traditional sit-up difficult. Here the emphasis is all on lowering the upper body, creating work for your abdominals but not straining your neck or shoulders.

1 Sit up with your feet on the floor in front of you with knees bent.

2 With your hands across your chest, breathe out and slowly lower your torso back to the floor over 10 seconds with full control. Unwind your spine one vertebra at a time.

3 Exhale and roll up to sitting again. If you're unable to raise back up, assist with your hands.

TIPS

Don't flop down or flatten your back – it should be a gentle, rolling movement. Keep the move continuous, slow on the way down, assisted on the way up, and don't rest on the floor. As you become stronger, slow the movement down.

Press-up

There's no better exercise to target your upper body in one single movement than the press-up. Arms, back, abdomen, shoulders and chest all get a workout. The chest is an area that is important to work, as the decollétage loses elasticity and firmness through lack of underlying muscle tone.

Basic press-up

1 Position your hands wide on the floor just below shoulder level. Don't allow your back or bottom to sag.

2 Slowly lower yourself in a plank movement until your chest is almost touching the floor.

3 Push yourself back up to the starting position.

TIPS

Don't fully extend your arms or allow them to lock out when pushing yourself back up.

Modified press-up

1 Kneel on the floor with your weight supported by your hands. Position your hands as for the basic press-up.

2 Lower your body to the floor. Your back, buttocks, neck and head should remain in a straight line.

3 Push yourself back up to the starting position.

TIPS

It's important not to hold your breath, drop your head or allow your lower back or pelvis to drop, causing your stomach to touch the floor. When at the lowest point of the movement, think of raising your bottom first to prevent your upper body coming up prematurely in a severe arch. The closer together the position of your arms, the harder your triceps will have to work, so as a chest exercise keep the hand position wide.

'There's no better exercise to target your upper body in one single movement than the press-up.'

Cardio pump II

Shoulder shaper

The turtle

Balance press-up

Stride jump

Posture press

Lower tummy tamer

Butt lifter II

Reverse
lunge/lift

Breast lift

Weights circuit

After the initial four-week cycle of the master plan,
you're ready to move up to this intermediate weights
circuit, also known as the 'sculpting' circuit because
it will tone and strengthen your muscles to give you
a firm, supple and great-looking body. At first,
you'll complete each activity at your own pace
for 30 seconds, twice a week for two weeks. Then,
for the following two weeks, you'll do 20 repetitions
of each activity instead of 30 seconds.

Cardio pump II

Perform the exercise as described on page 98, but using weights.

1 Begin climbing up the stairs two at a time until you reach the landing. Alternatively, use a secure box or step about 38 cm (15 in) high.

2 If there are further stairs on from here, continue climbing until you reach the top of the flight. If not, simply return to the bottom (taking one stair at a time) and then repeat for the allotted time.

3 As your fitness improves, increase your pace.

TIPS

Pay attention to your posture, avoiding looking down or slumping as you fatigue. Keep your back upright and tummy muscles tight. Don't hang on to the banister railing, or assist your legs by pushing down on the thighs with your hands.

Shoulder shaper

This move works at toning the arms and shoulders all at once. The shoulders rarely get worked through their full range of movement in our daily activities. One of the first things we look for when assessing a good physique is strong, straight shoulders. These will often slope down as we age and also through neglect. Firm, straight shoulders are also fundamental to the correct draping of clothes on your body.

1 Standing with a split stance or sitting on the stability ball with feet about shoulder-width apart on the floor, hold a pair of dumbbells at arm's length at your side.

2 Bring the dumbbells up in front in a smooth curve until they arrive in front of your shoulders, twisting inwards at the same time so that your palms now face in towards you. Without pausing, continue to push the dumbbells upwards until they arrive directly above your head, this time twisting outwards so that your palms now face forwards with the dumbbell handles end to end. Don't lock the elbows out at the top, and ensure that you exhale throughout the entire upwards movement.

3 Lower the dumbbells in exactly the reverse order, first to your shoulders, then down to your sides, breathing in as you do so.

4 Repeat without pausing.

TIPS

Keep the back arched with chest and head lifted high throughout the movement. If seated on the stability ball, keeping the legs out in front, rather than out wide to either side of the ball, will prevent excessive arching of the back, and will maintain the hips in the correct position. It will also add further challenge to the balancing muscles in your trunk and abdominals.

Butt lifter II

This is a variation on the simple Butt lifter (see pages 102–103) in which you perform the exercise carrying a light dumbbell in each hand. Don't forget to advance the exercise continually by increasing the weights.

Reverse lunge/lift

Most people have a dominant leg, one they use first when climbing stairs, or stepping out. Over time, this can cause injury and imbalances. As well as burning calories, this exercise helps with lower body balance and stability.

1 Stand upright with your feet shoulder-width apart. Take a deep breath and, with hands on the hips, take a large step back, landing on your toes.

2 Continue to lower your body until both legs are bent at right angles, with the back knee about 2.5 cm (1 in) off the floor (similar to the walking lunge, only in reverse).

3 Exhale as you drive off the rear foot, swinging it forwards and up, raising the knee in front of you. Inhale as you lower the knee and scoot the foot out to the rear again, landing on the toes in the rear lunge position as before.

4 Perform this move on the same leg 10 times, then swap legs.

TIPS

Keep your head up and look straight ahead to improve balance.

Breast lift

This is another great exercise for opening out and defining the chest. The décolletage is as much on display as the neck and face. The muscle tone and skin texture here need regular attention, and pectoral muscle toning with these exercises gives an ageless beauty. It also strengthens the front of the shoulder.

1 Take hold of the dumbbells and lie on a mat with knees bent at a right angle and feet flat on the floor.

2 Position the dumbbells above your body with your palms facing each other, with a very slight bend in the elbows. Squeeze the handles tightly.

3 Keeping the wrists and elbows in the same position, inhale deeply and lower the dumbbells wide and in a semicircular motion until the upper arms lightly touch the floor.

4 Feel the stretch and then exhale forcefully as you sweep upwards, bringing the dumbbells back around to their original position.

TIPS

It's important not to move the elbows from their rigid position when doing this exercise. New exercisers tend to bend their elbows, thus taking the work off the chest. Think of 'hugging' a tree.

Lower tummy tamer

Great for flattening the abdominals. Place your hands behind your head and lie on your back, placing the stability ball between your knees and shins. Curl your tail bone towards your navel as you lift the ball up, squeeze and extend your legs towards the ceiling as in the standard hip raise. On return, bring the ball down to about 45 degrees off the floor and repeat the movement without pausing. If you find this exercise difficult, you can perform a more basic version without the stability ball until you feel more comfortable with the movement.

> *Great for flattening the abdominals.*

1 Lying on the floor with the stability ball between your ankles, position your legs at 45 degrees to the floor, with a very slight, 'soft' bend in the knees.

2 With palms flat on the floor, breathe out and bring your legs up to a 90-degree position to the floor. At the same time continue to lift by squeezing your abdominals and glutes, lifting the pelvis upwards, raising the hips slightly off the floor.

3 Breathe in and lower your legs back down to 45 degrees, maintaining control throughout.

TIPS

Take care not to lower your legs so far down that the back arches – only to 45 degrees. Legs should never 'swing' back over the body when raising the hips. Drive straight up. Always keep a very slight bend in the knees so that you avoid lock-out. Try not to collapse, or 'crash', back down on to the floor – always exert control.

Posture press

Here's a great combination move to tone up the 'bat wings' (triceps) and for women to put some definition into the central back/shoulder area for the next time you're wearing a low-back or off-the-shoulder dress. Women are often plagued by skin creases over or under the bra strap across the central back or under the arms. This is where body fat will settle, but it also remains an untoned part of the body. Commonly, we do hours of cardio and other aerobic exercises to try to lose weight, but forget there are large muscle groups in our back that also need attention. A rounded back is detrimental to a healthy balance within the body and a youthful look.

1 Standing with a dumbbell in each hand at your side, with your feet about shoulder-width apart and knees very slightly bent, arch your back and lean forwards with your bottom sticking out.

2 Hold this position while you inhale and bring the dumbbells up against your side by the lower ribcage.

3 Hold the arms here and now exhale, extending your forearms out to the rear until the whole arm is pointing straight out behind you, and slightly high, in a continuous movement.

4 Reverse the movement, inhaling and exhaling in two parts as before, and repeat.

TIPS

Keep your head raised to ensure good posture and keep the airway open. Think of keeping the back arched throughout and bottom sticking out, but don't fully straighten the legs at any time.

Stride jump

This exercise comes straight out of basic military fitness, and we're going to use it to improve the shape of your calves, strengthen your hips and pelvis, and tone your shoulders. There is, of course, the added component of cardiovascular fitness to keep your heart rate up!

1 Standing on your toes with your arms by your sides, breathe out and leap up, landing with your left leg in front of you bent at a 90-degree angle and your right leg stretched out behind you with your heel raised. Land softly on the balls of the feet with the majority of your weight on the front leg. As you are leaping up and out with the legs, swing your right arm in front of you and your left arm behind.

2 Pause to breathe in. Breathe out forcefully as you leap up again, landing with both legs and arms in the opposite position.

TIPS

Ensure you land softly with knees flexed. For added effect, you can sink quite deeply in this movement before leaping up again but do not allow your front knee to protrude any further than the front foot. Keep your head up, tummy braced tightly and do not lean forward.

Balance press-up

More challenging than press-ups from the floor, using the stability ball in this exercise will help tighten up your obliques (the corset muscles around your waist) as you balance, pulling your stomach in from the sides as well as the front. Great target work to open up the chest, place the shoulders in good postural position and give the bust a natural lift.

1 Kneel behind the ball, then roll your body on top of it and forwards until it's directly under your knees.

2 Place your hands wider than shoulder-width apart as for a normal press-up, then proceed to bend at the elbow, lowering the chest towards the floor, inhaling as you do so.

3 Exhale and push your body up until your arms are just short of fully straight, then repeat the movement.

TIPS

Keep your head up, opening the airway, and use deep, full breaths to help drive the shoulders back into the correct position, avoiding a round-shouldered look. Keep your abdominals tight to control sideways movement from the ball, and don't sag in the middle!

The turtle

Here's a great one for strengthening up your back, buttocks and shoulders, giving a defined and athletic appearance at the same time. It's a favourite of our celebrity clients who are preparing to appear on the red carpet.

1 Lie relaxed prone (on your front) on the floor with arms extended out in front of you and legs together.

2 Inhale and raise your head, arms and legs just up off the floor. Sweep the arms around in a wide arc until your hands reach your sides. Squeeze the buttocks and thighs.

3 Exhale as you return to the original position, then repeat the movement, keeping your arms up off the floor at all times until finished.

TIPS

Use smooth movements, taking care not to 'jerk' or 'tug' on your lower back as you raise up or down. Keep your head and neck in neutral alignment.

‘ It's a favourite of our celebrity clients who are preparing to appear on the red carpet. ’

Sumo squat

Sissy squa

Manual
resistance

Neck toners

Jack hammer

Slouch adjustor

Target-toning programme

On the master plan, you should begin this target-toning programme alongside the weights circuit, performing it once a week for four weeks. It's a body-specific programme designed to concentrate on the areas that seem to trouble you most. It's not a circuit, but a conventional training workout where you perform the first activity 10 times, rest for 40 seconds and then do another set of 10. After another 40 seconds, you complete a third set of 10, before moving on to the next exercise on the list.

If you're not following the master plan, but simply want your body in amazing shape from top to toe, use this programme to zero in on your problem spots. Do the workout every second day for four weeks. Use the guidelines accompanying each exercise description to calculate which weight you should select for each exercise.

Butt blaster II

Advanced breast lift

Sumo squat

This exercise is fantastic for shaping and toning the buttocks and inner thighs, an area that presents many problems, including flabbiness, spider veins, fatty tissue and cellulite build-up. These squats bring a fresh blood supply to the area. Perform three sets of 12 repetitions. Rest for one minute between sets.

1 Stand up straight, facing away from a wall, with a stability ball against the wall and in the curvature of your lower back.

2 With your feet wide apart and your toes pointing outwards at about 45 degrees, fold your arms in front of you.

3 Keeping your chest up and shoulders back, inhale and bend your knees until the top of your thighs are parallel to the floor. Make sure your knees are wide and pointing over your second toes, and your back curves under the ball as you descend.

4 Breathe out and stand up to return to the starting position, keeping constant pressure against the ball throughout the movement. To make this really work well, concentrate on squeezing the buttocks hard as you come up.

TIPS

Take extra care not to lean forwards in this exercise. For best results, make sure your thighs and glutes do all the work. Warm up with some gentle squats without the ball for 12 repetitions. There should be no pain in the knees when doing this exercise. To progress, hold dumbbells in each hand down by your side while continuing the same movement. Increase the weight to keep progressing.

Sissy squat

This is an ideal exercise to bring knees back into shape and also work on the quadriceps, thighs and pelvic floor muscles. To give added benefit to the inner thigh, place a foam ball between your knees. Don't attempt this exercise if you have any knee pain, injuries or weaknesses. Beginners should start with one set of 8–10 repetitions. Work up to three sets. Rest for one minute between sets.

1 Hold on to a firm support and stand with your feet close together, and toes pointing slightly outwards.

2 Come up on to the balls of your feet, lean slightly backwards and lower your body. Before you descend, tilt your pelvis forwards, tighten and lift the pelvic floor area and tuck your glutes under. Stay on your toes as you go down. Try to go down with your shins parallel to the floor.

3 Pause at the bottom and, pressing through the balls of your feet, squeeze your thighs and buttocks and come up to the starting position again.

TIPS

Maintain the pelvic tilt and the buttock and pelvic floor squeeze at all times. If using a foam ball, or medicine ball, keep it firmly gripped between your thighs throughout the whole movement.

Butt blaster II

Nothing gets into the back of the upper thigh and that cellulite-prone area like this exercise. Our hamstrings are often a casualty of our sedentary lifestyles and it's the squeezing action of these muscles that helps take blood and lymph from the area. Working the hamstrings brings extra nutrients to the skin cells and helps flush away the toxic build-up that accumulates in this fat-prone area. As men get a double chin when they get fatter, so women get a 'double bum' with a secondary fat deposit just under the main buttock line. While it's impossible to spot-reduce fat, you can most certainly improve the tone of the muscles lying underneath. We sit for hours on end at a desk, in a car or in front of the television, and these muscles rarely get challenged, leaving the back of the leg untoned and flabby.

Beginners should perform one set of 12–16 repetitions; work up to three sets with a 30-second rest between sets.

'Nothing gets into the back of the upper thigh and that cellulite-prone area like this exercise.'

1 Stand upright with your feet shoulder-width apart, holding a pair of dumbbells by your sides. Keep your head up, your back straight and your shoulders pulled back.

2 Inhale as you allow your torso to slowly bend forwards and your hands to lower to just below your knees. Keep your head up, knees just slightly bent and maintain a tight arch in your lower back. Push your bottom out, with flat feet, but bodyweight pressed down through the heels.

3 Exhale and slowly lift your body back up to the starting position, keeping your hamstrings tensed and squeezing your buttocks tightly all the way up.

4 Lean back very slightly and lift the shoulders in a shrugging movement up behind your ears to complete the exercise.

TIPS

Sometimes it's useful to practise this movement side on to a mirror so you can check that your back doesn't 'round out' at the bottom of the movement. The spine must always be rigid with a firm arch, and there should always be a slight bend in the knee. You should feel this exercise in the mid-hamstring and buttocks. If you feel pain in the back of the knee, you may have your legs too straight.

Advanced breast lift

This version of the breast lift exercise (see page 113) targets the upper chest area, creating an attractive broad, smooth appearance to the décolletage. Most often when weight is lost quickly through crash dieting, this area ends up looking skinny, sunken and bony. Increase the weight as it becomes easier – remember to keep challenging yourself. Perform three sets of 12 repetitions. Rest for 30 seconds between sets.

1 Take hold of the dumbbells and lie on your back on a stability ball with legs bent at right angles and the ball supporting your head. Drop your bottom down so that the pelvis is lower than the chest, feet flat on the floor.

2 Position the dumbbells above your eyes with your palms facing each other with a very slight bend in the elbows. Squeeze the handles tightly.

3 Keeping the wrists and elbows in the same position, inhale deeply and sweep the dumbbells wide and down in a semicircular motion until the dumbbells are parallel to the shoulders. Don't go back any further.

4 Feel the stretch and then exhale as you sweep upwards, bringing the dumbbells back around to their original position.

TIPS

As with the breast lift exercise, it's important not to move the elbows from their rigid position. Again, think of 'hugging' a tree.

'Increase the weight as it becomes easier – remember to keep challenging yourself.'

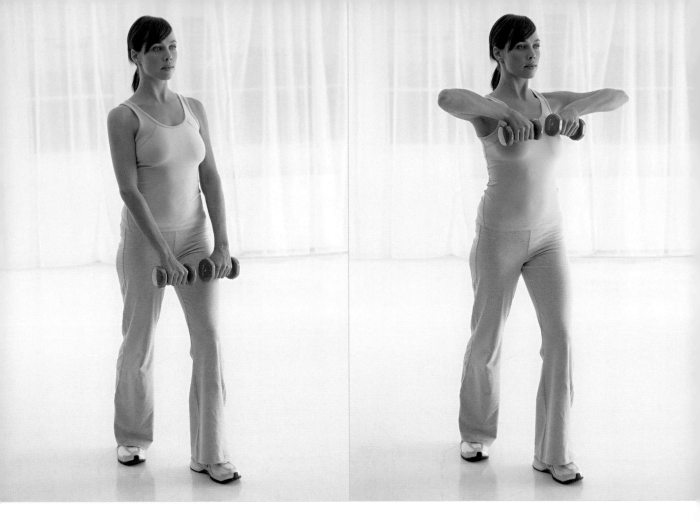

Slouch adjustor

An excellent exercise to correct rounded posture, this movement also gives a graceful and gently rising line from the shoulders to the neck.

1 Stand with feet shoulder-width apart, holding your weights close together. The arms are resting down against your thighs and your palms are facing in towards the body.

2 Lift your weights straight up to the upper chest until your elbows and forearms are parallel with the floor.

3 Lower to the starting point, resisting the weight.

TIPS

Make sure you do not sway your back when lifting the weights. Keep the spine and neck straight as you lower your arms. Feel it work into the back of the neck and shoulders as you lower your arms. Try not to slump the shoulders forwards. Keep your hands close together throughout the movement to work into this important postural muscle.

Jack hammer

For those who dislike exposing their arms in summer, this is an excellent exercise to tone up those flabby areas. Keep the fluid movement going, alternating arms for 15 repetitions on each.

1 Lying on the stability ball with your head supported, grasp a dumbbell in each hand with palms facing inwards, as if holding a hammer in each hand.

2 Keeping the elbows pointed at the ceiling, bring one dumbbell down beside your ear, then press back up to the original position.

3 Repeat with the other arm.

TIPS

Take care to control the movement, ensuring the dumbbells don't come too close to the side of your head. To create more definition and shape on the triceps, bring the arms further behind your head so that your elbows point out to the rear.

Neck toners

A long, graceful and flexible neck is an important part of looking great. These are exercises that are often forgotten in our efforts to improve body shape. If your jowls are beginning to sag and your chin is not as defined as it used to be, then these small muscles need a workout just as much as the larger ones. This is an area that is always on display – it needs balanced tightening and toning because it supports your head, which is heavy.

For safety's sake, when training the neck, it's extremely important to follow good form. Use smooth, controlled motion at all times; don't jerk or bounce at all.

Neck flexion Stand next to a wall or a pole and position the stability ball between this and your forehead. Bend your head and push into the ball as you exhale, feeling the tension from the chin to the neck. You may need to hold on to structural support for balance. Repeat the movement 8–10 times at a breathing pace.

Neck extension Facing the rear, place the back of your head against the ball, then press your head into the ball as you lift your chin and exhale. Don't move the rest of your body. Repeat the movement 8–10 times.

Manual resistance

You can use this exercise for training the front, back and both sides of your neck. A more advanced version is to allow your neck to move back and forth against the resistance, while keeping the resistance as high as possible.

1 Place the heel of one hand on the corresponding side of your head.

2 Apply pressure with your hand and resist with your neck. You can adjust the pressure according to your own strength. Press as hard as you can, as long as you are able to keep your neck still against the resistance. Repeat on the other side.

Glute muscle,
hip, chest and
forearm stretch

Calf, back and
arm stretch

Simple neck
stretches

Lower back
mobility stretch

Stretching

Stretching is an important part of any workout routine. It helps increase your flexibility and reduce your chances of injury. It's best to stretch the muscles you have used after you cool down; although, if you have any chronically tight muscles, you may want to stretch those after you warm up as well. Do each stretch at least once and hold for the specified number of seconds (more if you have time). Hold each stretch firmly and then push that little bit further as the muscle warms into the movement.

The stretching exercises on the next few pages should be undertaken in the order they appear, as each one follows on from the previous one.

Hamstring and lower back stretch

Inner thigh (adductor) stretch

Calf, back and arm stretch

1 From an even standing position, with the feet shoulder-width apart, drop the right foot back, and, keeping the leg straight, press the heel back and into the floor. At the same time, gently bend the front knee into a braced lunge to increase the stretch on the rear calf.

2 Clasping the fingers together, turn the hands inside out as you press upwards as high as you can with the arms fully extended. Bring the body fully upright, inhale deeply and hold your breath as you stretch upwards even higher.

3 Exhale and relax your body. Repeat, this time dropping the left foot back.

Glute muscle, hip, chest and forearm stretch

1 From the last position, bring the rear left leg forwards into an extended step, dropping immediately but smoothly into a deep lunge. Continue the movement forwards and down until the rear (right) knee gently rests on the floor.

2 Continue to sink forwards, leaning the body slightly to the rear, away from the front. At the same time raise both arms out to either side, turn the palms out and push back, inhaling deeply as you do so. Keep the head up, hold the breath in and then bend the fingers back. Hold for 5 seconds.

3 Exhale and relax your body. Repeat, this time bringing the right leg forwards.

Hamstring and lower back stretch

1 From the last position, slowly sit down on the floor and extend both legs straight out in front.

2 Stretch both arms out to reach down towards the toes and hold the furthest position you comfortably can as you exhale. You should feel tightness directly behind the knees. Don't bounce this (or any) stretch. Breathe lightly and hold for about 30 seconds.

3 Relax your body.

Inner thigh (adductor) stretch

1 From the last position, bring your feet in together and draw them closer to you with the soles flat against each other.

2 Placing the elbows on the inside of either knee, exhale and slowly lean forwards into the stretch, pushing the knees out and down towards the floor. Don't bounce this (or any) stretch. Breathe lightly and hold for about 30 seconds, maintaining a firm pressure against the knees.

3 Slowly bring your knees back towards each other.

Lower back mobility stretch

1 From the seated position of the last stretch, lie backwards on the floor with your knees tucked up at a right angle. Spread your arms out to either side and rest them on the floor.

2 Exhale as you slowly allow both knees to fall to one side, taking care that your shoulders remain in contact with the floor. Using shallow breaths, hold this for 30 seconds minimum. Allow the knees to get closer to the floor as you relax into the stretch.

3 Bring the knees up to a vertical position, and repeat the stretch on the other side.

Simple neck stretches

These exercises are meant to help you regain loss of movement in the neck region. Do each movement slowly five times, resting a short time in between each set of movements. Do them throughout the day.

1 Neck flexion

Bring your head forwards so that your chin hits your chest and your face is staring straight down at the floor.

2 Neck extension

Allow your head to go back until your face is looking directly at the ceiling. Note: if you feel dizzy when you do this, leave it out.

3 Neck rotation

Turn your head slowly round to one side until it cannot easily go any further. After five stretches repeat on the other side. (don't go from one side to the other or roll your neck about).

4 Side flexion

Keep your head facing straight forward and try to tip your ear down towards one shoulder. After five stretches repeat on the other side.

5 & 6 Forward flexion

This is one of the most useful neck movements, as it counteracts the tendency we all have of allowing our heads to poke forwards in a poor posture, and moves the upper cervical joints. Move your head forwards as far as you can, keeping your face pointing straight on, and then move your head back as far as it will go. This can also be done against a wall with the aid of a stability ball, as pictured. See page 130 for instructions.

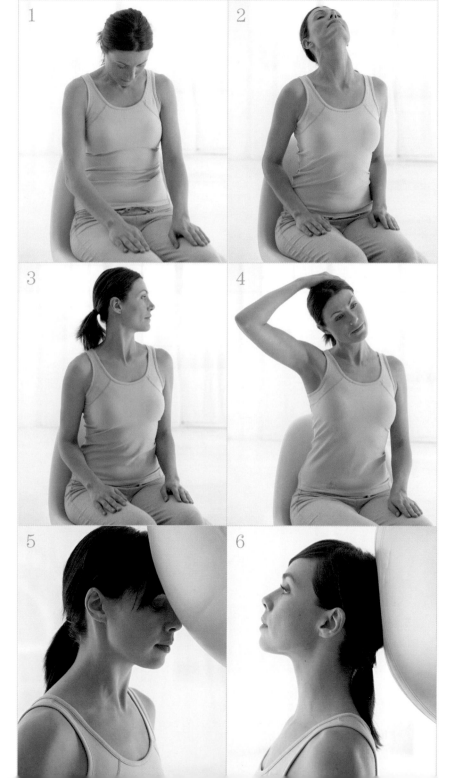

Index

Acknowledgements

To our wonderfully supportive children who have shared in this life long passion and to our parents who believed in the goodness of natural foods. Also for all our many, many clients who have had the determination and commitment to transform their physiques and their health... every one is an inspiration! Thank you also to Lisa and Jane at Hamlyn for all their help and assistance in guiding the ignorant, and to Nautilus for kindly supplying us with fitness equipment. A final thanks to a special client for her generosity in allowing her pictures to be used.

Your body is the ground and metaphor of your life, the expression of your existence. It is your Bible, your encyclopedia, your life story. Everything that happens to you is stored and reflected in your body. In the marriage of flesh and spirit divorce is impossible.
Gabrielle Roth

If you have enjoyed this book, look on our website for more exclusive content. Simply log on to **www.turnbackyourageclock.com** and enter the password **tbyac**.

Other places to visit to find out more information about us, our speaking, seminars and live events:
www.iopm.co.uk
www.timbean.com

PICTURE CREDITS
Commissioned Photography:
© **Octopus Publishing Group Limited**/Russell Sadur

Other Photography:
Alamy/Tetra Images 22
Corbis 14; /Jutta Klee 59; /Tim Pannell 17; /Tom Grill 8
Octopus Publishing Group Limited/Gareth Sambidge 44; /Gary Latham 72 bottom; /Lis Parsons 66; /Peter Pugh-Cook 58, 80; /Russell Sadur 7, 68, 90; /Ruth Jenkinson 62; /William Lingwood 74; /William Reavell 16, 71, 72 top

Royalty-Free Images/Getty Images 15; /imagesource 2, 21; /PhotoDisc 6, 81, 87; /Photolibrary 91
Shutterstock/Emin Kuliyev 69

PUBLISHER'S ACKNOWLEDGEMENTS
Executive Editor Jane McIntosh
Senior Editor Lisa John
Executive Art Editors Joanna MacGregor and Mark Stevens
Designer Geoff Borin
Senior Production Controller Martin Croshaw